Praise for "L.I.F.E"

"An inspiring and thoughtful book. One that will eventually impact the lives of millions.

Ken Brown explains in the most simple terms how to live a life worth living. Thanks to **'Living In Freedom Everyday'**, I now realize that a career is what you're paid for but a calling is what you're made for. Read this book and discover what you are called to do."

- **DENNIS KIMBRO, AUTHOR**
Think & Grow Rich: A Black Choice and
What Makes the Great Great

Ken Brown is to be commended for writing an honest, exciting, informative   treatment of personal success principles. Ken's first hand treatment of personal experiences and life lessons gained in his rise from poverty to prominence says "you can do it too". He illustrates his success principles of faith, vision, purpose, passion, ownership, and associations through the lives of other achievers who used these principles to overcome great odds and realize their visions. Biblical references and illustrations add another dimension to Ken's message. Reading **L.I.F.E** will undoubtedly rekindle the desire of many readers to study the Bible and implement its principles in their lives. Ken Brown has given a very practical meaning to the concept of **L.I.F.E., Living In Freedom Everyday**. This book is a personal blueprint for massive success.

- **HERBERT HARRIS, AUTHOR**
The Twelve Universal Laws of Success

"This is one the best books I've read this year. This is best seller material. The way in which it combined faith, practical advice and personal experience makes it so easy and enjoyable to read. Everyone who reads it will be blessed and encouraged. I know I was."

- DEIDRE BROWN
Vice President, Brown Food Group Inc.

"Wow! I simply love this book. I couldn't put it down once I started it. Seldom does a book say it better or more simply than **L.I.F.E: Living In Freedom Everyday**. This book is a must read for all those who are serious about leading a fulfilling and productive life. My heartfelt thanks goes out to Kenneth Brown for giving us a gem."

- GEORGE C. FRASER, AUTHOR
CLICK: Ten Truths For Building Extraordinary Relationships

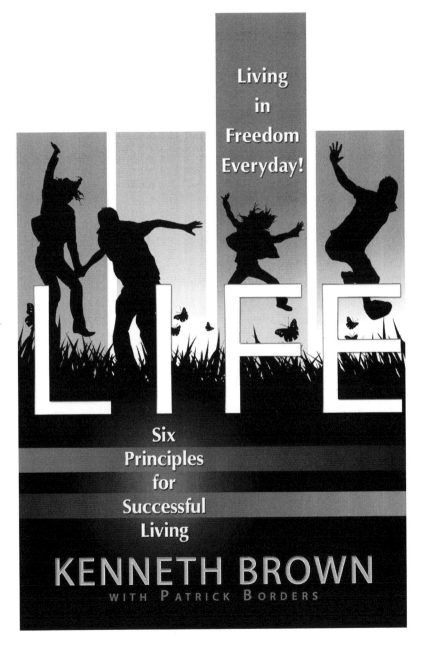

LIFE

Living in Freedom Everyday!

Six Principles for Successful Living

KENNETH BROWN

WITH PATRICK BORDERS

Ken Brown International • Walled Lake, Michigan

L.I.F.E.
SIX PRINCIPLES FOR
LIVING IN FREEDOM EVERYDAY

Unless otherwise noted, all scripture quotations
are taken from the NKJV of the Holy Bible.

ISBN (13) 978-0-9768742-5-6

Cover and Interior Design: Selah Branding and Design, LLC

Edited by Patrick Borders and Skyla P. Thomas

Ken Brown International • Walled Lake, Michigan

Printed in the United States of America

DEDICATION

I WISH TO DEDICATE THIS BOOK

TO MY CARING, GIVING AND LOVING PARENTS,

JOHN AND **REGINA BROWN.**

THEY TAUGHT ME TO KNOCK,

SEEK AND TO FIND TRUTH IN EVERY

AREA OF MY LIFE. I WISH TO DEDICATE

THIS BOOK TO THE LEGACY THEY LEAVE BEHIND-

A LEGACY OF OUTRAGEOUS FAITH, ABSOLUTE

EXCELLENCE AND GIVING FOR A LIVING.

Acknowledgements

To My Wife **Deidre** and Sons
Austin, Bradley and **Drake.**
Thank you for allowing,
encouraging and inspiring me
to Live In Freedom Every Day....

TABLE OF CONTENTS

INTRODUCTION - A MORE ABUNDANT LIFE

FAITH– PART ONE

VISION – PART TWO

PURPOSE – PART THREE

PASSION – PART FOUR

OWNERSHIP-PART FIVE

ASSOCIATIONS – PART SIX

INTRODUCTION

A MORE ABUNDANT LIFE

The first time I met Tawana Williams, I was sitting in the front row of an auditorium while participating in a Les Brown speaker training conference. I was listening to a presentation, and at the end of it, the speaker offered to answer questions from the audience. Someone in the back raised her hand, and the speaker called on her.

I turned around to see the questioner but couldn't spot her behind the rows of people. I don't remember what she asked, but I do remember the energy and passion in her voice.

It was customary at this conference for a questioner to stand, and I guess other people couldn't see her either, because someone in the audience interrupted and asked her to stand.

"I *am* standing," came the voice behind the rows. "But I'll move into the aisle, so you can see me."

A woman who stood less than five feet tall stepped into the aisle. But her size wasn't the first thing I noticed. The woman had no arms. Nothing below her shoulders.

The next day, I had the pleasure of sitting next to that woman, Tawana Williams. We were listening to another speaker, and I was taking notes, when I noticed Tawana moving one of her legs. I glanced to the floor and noticed she was taking notes with her foot. Not only was she taking notes, she wrote faster than I and with beautiful penmanship. Every i was dotted; every t crossed. She didn't miss a beat. She put me to shame.

After meeting at that conference, Tawana and I became close friends. I learned she was also a motivational speaker, and since then, we've spoken together at various seminars. She travels the country talking to groups—

inspiring people with her passion for life and her dedication to overcoming all obstacles put in her way. She's married to a tall, handsome man. She's raised a beautiful child. She has a wonderful home that's been featured in *Homes of Color*.

She's successful. And she's living in freedom.

Tawana could have dwelled in a lifelong pity party. Instead, she set her mind to living an abundant life and shining her light for others. She's on fire.

Unfortunately, too many of us are not living in freedom although we long to be. We long to have joy. We long to follow God's calling. But we're stuck. We can't seem to move to the next level, and every time we try, we get smacked down to where we started.

Another acquaintance of mine, Derrick, knows what it means to be stuck. Most of his life had been perfect. He married his high school sweetheart, and they had several beautiful children. He owned a nice home, and for a while, he had a good job. His wife loved all the things he provided.

During the first 10 years of his job, he earned several promotions. But then he hit a ceiling and his career stalled. He started to hate his job, but he didn't know what to do to solve the problem.

He grew more and more depressed. At first, his wife supported him and tried to encourage him. But eventually, his all-consuming depression grew too much for her. She filed for divorce.

It didn't take long before his ex-wife met someone new, got married, and had more children. She moved on with her life.

But Derrick didn't. He was trapped. He couldn't accept that she had left him. For a while, he waited for her to come back, but when it was obvious she wasn't, his depression turned to resentment and anger. "Women are terrible," he told me.

I tried to lift him up. "This is a time to make a clean start," I said. "You're not obligated to support her financially any longer. Now you can pursue what you really want to do in life. You can find a new vision for your life." He had an opportunity to find a new mate, I told him. "You can find someone who's better suited for your new vision."

But he wouldn't move. He stagnated—dwelling in a world of blame and hopelessness.

Why is it that so many of us are enslaved to the events of life, while others, like Tawana, are able to live in freedom?

As a speaker and a life coach, I work with many people who struggle with this thing called life. I work with the CEO who controls countless employees and gobs of money, but spends no time with his family and suffers from stress-related health problems. I work with the housewife who gets up every morning to take care of her husband and children but constantly wonders, *Is there anything more to life than this?* I work with the teacher who has earned the education degrees and has accumulated years of experience, but has lost the fire and simply goes through the paces.

I work with people who view life as a series of circumstances and problems that control them. But life isn't about being controlled by outside influences. *Jesus said that He came that we "may have life" and "have it more abundantly."*[1] Abundant life is not about being a slave to external desires and events. Abundant life, or L.I.F.E., if you will, is about Living In Freedom Everyday. It's about shaking free of the shackles that bind us and breathing in the spirit of freedom.

Many of us don't realize, however, that although we broke the bonds of slavery a century and a half ago, we've voluntarily entered a new phase of slavery. Harriet Tubman once complained, *"If I could have convinced more more slaves that they were slaves, I could have freed more."* Many people today need to realize the reality of their new slavery.

We're slaves to a job we don't like or to a job that forces us into an unbalanced lifestyle. We're in bondage to bills that keep us up at night with worries. We're hooked on alcohol or drugs or bad relationships. There are hundreds of ways we get stuck in life instead of living in freedom.

It's not supposed to be that way. God created us as masters. He created us to have "dominion . . . over all the earth."[2] But instead, we look in the mirror and ask, "How did my problems get bigger than me?"

How did it happen? It happened by looking outside ourselves for happiness. Life, as it turns out, is an inside job. Success is an inside job. Joy is an inside job. We look for other people, places, and things to make us happy, and sometimes, for a brief period of time, they do. However, just as the word *happy* is related to the word *happening*, happiness requires certain external things happening over and over again. Happiness is a slave to other things outside our control.

Joy is different. Joy comes from inside. It comes from our faith in God. It comes from our desire to follow Christ. It comes from our belief in who we are—our belief that we're God's unique masterpieces meant to live life abundantly and in freedom.

Joy doesn't depend on the weather; it doesn't depend on the economy. It doesn't care who's in the White House.

When we live in slavery, problems follow us. But when we live in freedom, success follows us. That doesn't mean that things will all of sudden become easy—that riches will fall into our laps from heaven. True success isn't about achieving a certain level of wealth. It's not about amassing more degrees than on a thermostat. It's not about having a spouse or children that make us feel good about ourselves. As Jesus says, "For what profit is it to a man if he gains the whole world, and loses his own soul?"[3]

Too often we live for some distant moment when we'll "gain the whole world." But *freedom isn't lived for the moment but in all moments.* True freedom isn't even a specific destination. It's a journey.

An old saying that often gets passed around by e-mail goes: "The road of success is not straight. There's a curve called failure, a loop called confusion, speed bumps called friends, red lights called enemies, caution lights called family. You will have flats called jobs. But if you have a spare called determination, an engine called perseverance, insurance called faith, and a driver called Jesus, you'll make it to your destiny." Although we'll, no doubt, find the success God has in mind for us, it's in those moments of faith, perseverance, determination, and most important, dependence on Christ that we'll discover our freedom.

We must remember that a sacrifice has been made for us. Jesus went to the cross so we could enjoy the life that God has ordained. In Galatians 5:1, Paul tells us: "Stand fast therefore in the liberty by which Christ has made us free, and do not be entangled again with a yoke of bondage."

With faith in God, and a desire to pursue Christ's gift of freedom, how do we step out and take dominion over that freedom? That's what this book will answer.

Through my own life experiences—my own traps in the business rat race and my own choices to discover "the more" of life—and through my experiences as a life coach, I've formulated six principles that will propel you along the road of success. To live in freedom, we each must have *faith, vision, purpose,* and *passion.* In addition, we must take *ownership* of our lives and *associate* ourselves with people who will lift us up and not keep us down.

Faith

Before anything else, we must exhibit faith in God. Faith is the absolute cornerstone through which we achieve a free life. Through a total belief in the sovereignty of God, we can find the power to overcome barriers and succeed.

When our brain tells us no, when our situation tells us success is impossible, faith steps in and removes doubt. It is the "substance of things hoped for, the evidence of things not seen."[4] We might not wield absolute control over our circumstances, but the Lord wields absolute control to achieve whatever He wants to achieve through us.

Vision

What does success look like to you? Have you crystallized a vision of a free life? To be honest, I don't think the typical person has spent much effort contemplating and discerning a vision of success. They might assign a dollar figure to success, but money is the by-product of success; it's not the goal, and it's certainly not the vision.

Like using a camera lens, we must focus to have proper vision. Otherwise, as Proverbs 29:18 says: "Where there is no vision, the people perish." Without vision, we simply walk in darkness, stumbling along as life's events bump us from one obstacle to another. But with vision—spiritual vision that is—we can see the invisible and do the impossible.

Purpose

Purpose is closely related to vision but is more concrete. It's the *why* for living. Why were you sent here? What will be your legacy—your footprint on the world? What goals are you striving for that result in a journey of success and a life of significance?

Your purpose is ordained by God and is not determined by a desire for money or other external attractions. Your life is not for you but is for something higher. It's not for you, but *it is* up to you. You're to direct your talents and time to improving the lives of other people.

Passion

Once you understand your purpose, it will naturally lead to passion. Passion manifests itself in boundless enthusiasm. It gives you the energy you need to seek the impossible and the determination you need to overcome the roadblocks that obstruct your road to success.

Passion gives you a positive, unwavering attitude, and as we've often heard, your attitude will determine your altitude. As Henry Ford said about attitude: "Whether you think you can or you think you can't, you're right."

Ownership

Ownership is about doing all you can, with all you have, from the place you are. George Bernard Shaw once said: "The people who get on in this world are the people who get up and look for the circumstances they want. And if they can't find them, they make them."

When we own up to our lives, we don't indulge in blaming others. We assume 100 percent responsibility for our thoughts and actions. We understand that a free life is created from the power to choose and from taking ownership of our choices.

Associations

Have you seen photographs of couples who, after decades of marriage, start to resemble each other? They've spent so much time together that they look alike and act alike. When it comes to our friends and close associates, we may not look alike, but as it relates to our level of freedom, we become the people we hang with.

Our environment, meaning our family and friend-ship influences, can be stronger than our will to succeed. Jesus tells us not to "cast our pearls before swine."[5] To climb to the next level, we must foster associations with people who will nurture our aspirations.

In the following chapters, we'll take a close look at each of these six principles—exploring what they mean in greater detail and what practical steps you can take to succeed at each of them.

By adhering to these principles, we'll discover how people like Tawana Williams manage to live in freedom despite enormous obstacles. And we'll discover how to live the abundant life that Christ so desperately longs for each of us to enjoy.

(Footnotes)
All Scripture passages are from the
New King James Version unless otherwise noted.

[1] John 10:10
[2] Genesis 1:26
[3] Matthew 16:26
[4] Hebrews 11:1
[5] Matthew 7:6

FAITH

PART ONE

CHAPTER 1

Faith is the Foundation

The Lord had led Moses and the Israelites out of slavery. He had performed one of the most impressive miracles of all time, parting the Red Sea and directing the Israelites through that avenue of escape. During their journey, God provided them with water. He provided them with food. He provided them with victory in battle.

Finally, He led them to the doorstep of the Promised Land. Before letting them enter, however, the Lord instructed Moses to order twelve leaders, one from each tribe, to spy out the land of Canaan. Moses commanded them to discover the characteristics of the land and its people and to bring back a report.[1]

When the spies returned, they brought mixed news. The land, they said, "truly flows with milk and honey . . . Nevertheless the people who dwell in the land are strong; the cities are fortified and very large."

Two of the twelve spies, Caleb and Joshua, wanted to take possession of the land immediately, but the other ten wanted nothing doing. "We are not able to go up against the people, for they are stronger than we," they said. To the ten, the Canaan inhabitants looked like giants: "We were like grasshoppers in our own sight."

Upon hearing that, the Israelites lost their faith and wept with fear. "Would it not be better for us to return to Egypt?" they asked.

Joshua tried to encourage them. "If the LORD delights in us, then He will bring us into this land and give it to us." Don't fear the inhabitants of the land he told them.

The people refused to believe, however. So, the Lord punished them for their unbelief. He sentenced them to wander the desert for forty years until a new generation could be raised up to enter the Promised Land.

As readers of the Bible, it's easy for us to condemn the Israelites for their lack of faith. God took such good care of them, yet they didn't possess the faith necessary to experience true freedom. They'd escaped slavery, and the Lord had promised them a land flowing with milk and honey. He'd pointed them toward success, but the people were too afraid to believe it was possible. They were too afraid to believe God could overcome the appearance of impossible obstacles—the giant inhabitants of the land.

Instead of entering the land of promise, they desired to return to the land of slavery. They desired to return to their comfort zone. Without faith, they could never climb to the next level, so they might as well go back to the place where they were "stuck" for so long.

Yes, it's easy to judge them. But many of us face the same struggle. God has a promised land assigned for each of us, but we lack the faith to follow Him there. We lack the faith to achieve success and climb to the next level of our lives. We see ourselves as grasshoppers looking up in worry and resignation to the giants of our obstacles.

Success Is an Inside Job

Some people declare that a business degree is a requirement for achieving success in the business world. Other people declare that the guidance of loving, attentive parents is a requirement for ultimately finding success in our adult relationships. Experts propose countless "requirements" we must have to obtain success, but in the end, there's really only one requirement for success: faith. Success cannot happen without faith in God. Living in freedom cannot happen without faith in God. Everything else is built upon its foundation: your job, your business, your family, your relationships.

SUCCESS CANNOT HAPPEN WITHOUT FAITH IN GOD

Jesus tells us that a person of faith is "like a man building a house, who dug deep and laid the foundation on the rock. And when the flood arose, the stream beat vehemently against that house, and could not shake it, for it was founded on the rock. But he who heard and did nothing is like a man who built a house on the earth without a foundation, against which the stream beat vehemently; and immediately it fell. And the ruin of that house was great."[2]

When we build our job, business, family, and relationships on the foundation of faith, they are able to withstand any situation—any tragedy, any economy, or any obstacle that would derail the dreams of people without faith.

If you're preparing to take the next step in your life—like starting a business or getting married—I'd like to offer you congratulations. And also a word of warning. Before you make the leap, you must inspect yourself. Do you believe that God will lead you to success? Do you have the faith to follow Him in the freedom that He ordains for you?

I MADE A COMMITMENT TO GET TO KNOW CHRIST

If your faith is not yet strong, if you have fear and doubts, if you don't spend time in prayer and the Word, then I encourage you to realign your priorities. Your first step in pursuing the next level is not a business plan. It's not a marriage proposal. It's not something you do externally, but instead, it's something you do deep inside.

You must "seek first the kingdom of God and His righteousness, and all these things shall be added to you."[3] By pursuing the Lord first, then you'll be prepared to receive the abundance that He has promised.

Faith is deeply personal. And as such, it's difficult to write about. I can't summarize your personal faith for you in words. I can't draw a picture of it. I can't quote experts that will give you a concise definition. I can't give it to you in any form. It can only be discovered through the mystery of an intimate relationship with our Lord.

If you've read my book, *From Welfare to Faring Well*, then you might recall my mother's deep faith. Her faith impacted me tremendously, and it's one of the reasons I've taken a positive outlook on life. But she didn't give me my faith. As a child, I went to church all the time; however, the pastors I heard couldn't give me my faith, either. I didn't truly believe until I sought a personal relationship with Jesus Christ. I made a commitment to get to know Christ, and as that relationship developed, the faith that says "all things are possible" grew inside of me.

Each of us possesses the power to succeed. As a speaker and life coach, I'm glad people ask me for assistance, and I believe I help them, but I succeed by putting people in touch with the power they already possess. Many people read books, listen to tapes, and attend speeches in an attempt to use outside influences to discover the secret to a free life. But it's Jesus Christ inside of us that sets us free.

Without faith, we're like Israelites wandering the desert. We're not living life; life is living us. Proverbs 22:4 says that "by humility and the fear of the Lord are riches and honor and life." Through humbleness and respect, we recognize the overwhelming sovereignty of God. And through our faith, we receive heavenly riches, divine honor, and a life of freedom.

Plans to Prosper You

Our faith faces one of its toughest challenges when confronted with our desire to know the future. We want to know what's going to happen, and because we don't know, we doubt God's given our future much thought. But the Lord has a very specific life-design for each of us.

Just as faith is very personal, success is very personal as well. "'For I know the plans I have for you,' declares the LORD, 'plans to prosper you and not to harm you, plans to give you hope and a future.'"[4] He wants us to be prosperous in life. He wants us to be whole.

We must understand, however, that God has good

reasons for not divulging too much of His plans. The Word says that the "eye has not seen, nor ear heard, nor have entered into the heart of man the things which God has prepared for those who love Him."[5] We cannot enter into the Lord's mind. We can't conceive of what He has in the making. If He did share His plans with us, we'd crumble under the enormity of it.

We wouldn't be able to handle it for the same reason that gaining wealth through the lottery doesn't work. When people win the lottery, they end up less happy than before they won. Often, they end up losing all their winnings. They're not ready for the windfall; what they reaped in riches, they didn't sow in preparation. With us, God has to build us up gradually—teaching us through experience and testing us through challenges.

God has "set eternity in the hearts of men; yet they cannot fathom what God has done from beginning to end."[6] We cannot know the details of all God's plans, but faith does allow us the special insight we need to obtain wholeness.

Success in life—as God would define it—has little to do with money and everything to do with wholeness, with healing. It means we live a life free from the spiritual ailments that keep us enslaved.

When we read about stories of healing in the Gospels, it's easy to spot a commonality. When the centurion asked Jesus to heal his servant and believed Jesus could even heal him from a distance, Jesus said, "Go your way; and as you have believed, so let it be done for you."[7] When the woman who suffered from the flow of blood for twelve years reached out and touched the hem of Jesus' garment, Jesus responded, "Daughter, be of good cheer; your faith has made you well. Go in peace."[8] When the four friends brought the paralytic to Jesus by lowering him through a roof, "Jesus saw their faith." He told the paralytic, "Son, your sins are forgiven you," and He healed him.[9]

Jesus delivered physical freedom to those people for one simple reason: they believed. They believed in the awesome power of God. In the same way, if we express the same faith, Jesus will also deliver freedom by healing us from our spiritual ailments.

If faith is the answer, however, why don't we just hop on board and have perfect faith? The enemy of faith, namely fear, gets in the way. Fear and faith cannot coexist. We must commit ourselves to one or the other.

FAITH AND FEAR CANNOT CO-EXIST

The cancers in our mind—our doubts and worries, our fears—destroy our success. But fear actually represents nothing more than False Expectations Appearing Real. We think the Promised Land is inhabited by giants—that there's no way we can defeat them. We think we're as small as grasshoppers. We think our lives would be better in slavery.

Recently, I coached Michael, a man who dreamed of owning his first home. But he was too afraid to act on his dream. Every time I suggested he take a concrete step, he avoided it. He was stuck.

Finally, he admitted his reason for avoidance. His credit score was too low to get a mortgage, he claimed.

Curious, I asked him what the score was.

"I don't know," he said.

"Then how do you know it's too low?"

"I just know it is. Given my past, there's no way it's

good enough."

Fear held him back. He hadn't checked the score in five years, and he had false expectations that appeared as real.

Eventually, I persuaded him to obtain his score. It turned out to be 700—more than enough for his dream. Like the Israelites who viewed themselves as grasshoppers, Michael created a false roadblock and shrank to the size of his problem. Michael had talked himself out of success.

We must choose between fear and faith, because one of those will control our thoughts. Our thoughts control our words; our words control our actions; our actions control our character, and our character controls our destiny.

When we recognize fear for the imposter it is, and replace negative thoughts with a commitment to faith, we gain insights into God's plan. We see the vision He's trying to show us. And we position ourselves to confront the challenges that test our desire for our personal Promised Land.

In trying to live a life of faith, we have no better role model than Paul. In Acts, we see him preparing to leave Asia and bidding farewell to the elders of Ephesus. As I've mentioned, success is a journey and not a destination, and in Paul, we see this as a literal truth. He traveled great distances to spread the gospel.

In his farewell, Paul says: "Now I go bound in the spirit to Jerusalem, not knowing the things that will happen to me there, except that the Holy Spirit testifies in every city, saying that chains and tribulations await me."[10]

Through a great faith in Christ Jesus, however, the challenges that awaited Paul didn't even register as a concern. "None of these things move me; nor do I count my life dear to myself, so that I may finish my race with joy, and the ministry which I received from the Lord Jesus, to testify to the gospel of the grace of God."[11] Paul knew God had plans for him, and he didn't worry over what might happen. He was filled with faith and vision.

With faith, the joy of fulfilling our assignment will move us, and the challenges that await us will not. We will enter our Promised Land and enjoy the abundant grace of God.

(Footnotes)
[1] Numbers 13-14
[2] Luke 6:48-49
[3] Matthew 6:33
[4] Jeremiah 29:11 (NIV)
[5] 1 Corinthians 2:9
[6] Ecclesiastes 3:11
[7] Matthew 8:13
[8] Luke 8:48
[9] Mark 2:5
[10] Acts 20:22-23
[11] Acts 20:24

CHAPTER 2

Walking While Blindfolded

A few months ago, my family and I celebrated Father's Day with a candlelit picnic dinner served with an appetizer of faith.

It was raining that day, and I was in our basement reading when my wife, Deidre, and my three sons called me to the top of the stairs.

"Why?" I asked, not wanting to leave a good book.

"Never mind why," Dee said. "Just come up."

When I arrived at the top, they told me to close my eyes. I obeyed.

Then they wrapped a blindfold around my eyes and something strange happened. Anxiety took over. I froze. Although I was safely in my home, I felt incredibly uncomfortable.

My wife took one of my arms and Bradley the other. "Come with us," they said.

But I was paralyzed. I couldn't move. I'm not sure

what I thought would happen, but without my eyesight, I simply didn't believe I could get where I was supposed to go. I stood as rigid as a soldier.

"It's okay," Dee said. "We've got you."

"Come on, Dad," Bradley said.

I took one hesitant step and then another. "That's it," Dee said. "You're doing good."

GOD REQUIRES OUR OBEDIENCE IN ORDER FOR US TO MOVE FORWARD

Unable to use my eyes, I tried to form a picture in my mind of where I was headed. I also knew, without a doubt, that I could trust my family to lead me.

With each step, I relaxed, turning a corner here, turning a corner there. Eventually, we came to a stop, and Dee pulled off the blindfold. Presented before me was our garage, but on this day, it was no ordinary garage.

Dee had pulled her car out, and in its place was the patio table adorned with candles, fancy dinnerware, black and gold decorations, and a picnic fit for a king. My family had prepared a feast for the eyes.

Our experiences of faith mirror my blindfold experience. We can't see the path ahead, and in the end, God requires our obedience in order for us to move forward. I didn't have faith while walking blindfolded because I had never done it before. I didn't know how to do it; I didn't know where I was going. But in order to move, I had to step out despite my lack of eyesight.

I followed Deidre because I respected her control over the situation. I knew she could be trusted, just as a soldier obeys his commanding officer because the officer earned the right to be trusted. When the officer commands the soldier to move out, he doesn't stand around debating the order in his head. He doesn't say, "Tell me where I'm moving out first." He just does it.

But who is this God that we're supposed to obey? And has He earned our trust? This God we're supposed to obey is the same God who created the universe—the world and everything in it—in six days. He's the God that led Abraham, Isaac, and Jacob. He's the God that begat the Savior of the world. He's the God that created you and me. He's the God that saves each of us, time and time again.

Yes, I'd say He's earned our trust. If He's going to take us blindly down unfamiliar paths, then the least we can do is recognize we couldn't be in better hands. Following Him is the right thing to do. He has enough of a track record.

Planting a Seed

My friend Stephan has a dog, and once when I visited Stephan, I tried to get the dog to sit. "Sit, China, sit," I said. But she just ignored me and turned away. Of course, when Stephan walked by, he told China to sit and her rear-end hit the floor. Stephan had a track record with China, and she knew Stephan had, and would, take good care of her. China also knew that Stephan offered benefits for her obedience and consequences for any defiance.

Children obey their parents because their parents have a track record with them as well. A mom can place her baby on a table and change his diaper while the baby barely pays attention. But when a stranger baby-sits and changes the diaper, the baby stares wide-eyed and curious, trying to determine if the adult can be trusted.

When a healthy relationship exists, it enables trust to build and faith to grow. The same thing is true with

Jesus—when we're in a relationship with Him, when we have an intimate connection, we trust Him.

As with my blindfold experience, faith doesn't involve seeing with your eyes, but seeing with your mind. It's picturing the impossible and knowing that "all things are possible to him who believes."[1] No one is born without the potential for sufficient faith.

If you think about it, everyone has faith to some degree. How many of us test-drive a car and take it out on the highway, putting the pedal to the metal. We open her up. Imperfect human beings put that car together piece by piece, yet we still have faith that it won't fall apart at 90 mph—that the steering wheel will steer and the brake pedal will brake. We board a plane and trust that it won't fall apart in mid-air. We use electrical appliances and trust that they've been wired correctly and won't electrocute us.

So, if God deserves our faith because of his track record and universe-creating power, and we already believe in other things, then logically, we're ready to start our journey of faith.

And it really takes very little faith to begin. Everything you need is already inside of you. When you plant a garden, you put a seed in the ground and then you nurture it—you fertilize it; you water it. When you accept that God created you as a unique masterpiece, you'll find the unique gifts that lay buried within you, and you'll believe you can use those gifts to live a free life.

Your first step is to obey and to use that tiny flicker of faith. That tiny flicker will be enough. Jesus said as much when he said, "The kingdom of heaven is like a mustard seed, which a man took and sowed in his field, which indeed is the least of all the seeds; but when it is grown it is greater than the herbs and becomes a tree, so that the birds of the air come and nest in its branches."[2]

Faith doesn't require our brains, our problem-solving abilities. When we can't figure out our problems logically, we can turn to our heart—the home of our faith. That's where you can nurture the radical belief that all things are possible.

When you're blindfolded, you take the first step in obedience. When you notice that the step worked, then your faith grows. You take more steps, constantly following Jesus as He shows you the way. As that seed of faith is nurtured, it grows into something large and secure.

FAITH PROMPTS US TO ACT

Faith prompts us to act—but to act in a way that often seems illogical to the earthly world. When the woman who had bled for twelve years reached out for Jesus' garment, it was faith that compelled her to act. She hadn't seen Jesus before, but when He walked by, she believed. We can imagine that spirit of faith growing within her heart until she spontaneously reached out to touch His clothes. The crowd around her must have thought she was nuts, but her faith healed her anyway.

Call to Activate

I mentioned in the last chapter how I couldn't inherit my faith from my mother or my pastors. I did see how it worked, however. I saw the dreams my mother believed in—the dreams of a home, of her children getting an education. When I witnessed those things manifested, I said to myself, "Wow. This faith stuff works. I don't know how, but it works."

Logically, I knew there was something to it. I kept

attending church as I grew up. I could talk like a Christian. Shout like a Christian. Dress like a Christian. But it wasn't until I spent time with Jesus that I opened my heart. And when I opened my heart, something supernatural took over. I truly believed Christ Jesus could do anything with me that He wanted.

When we act without faith, it's like being blindfolded and playing pin-the-tail-on-the-donkey. We have no guide, and we're spun around several times. We almost always miss our goal.

IT WAS ONLY THROUGH KINGDOM CURRENCY THAT MY DREAM CAME TRUE

When we invest a bunch of money in some scheme because we want to be rich, we use earthly currency in a blind attempt to attain our dreams. But faith is the currency of God's kingdom. It's a currency that grows as long as you nurture it. And it's a currency that can be used to achieve infinitely more than earthly currency can.

For most of my adult life, I knew I wanted to start my own business. I believed I could do it, and I believed God had ordained my owning a business someday. But I didn't possess the money to make it work. In fact, I once tried to purchase a restaurant by borrowing money from my extended family by using earthly currency. But they didn't buy into my dream, and the deal fell through.

I continued to grow in my faith, however, and I still believed I'd one day own a restaurant. I worked for several food industry companies, gaining experience. I worked my way up the McDonald's company, gaining invaluable experience there also.

Then, when God knew I was ready, McDonald's offered me a loan to buy two franchises in Detroit. Before I knew it, I was an entrepreneur and an employer to more than one hundred workers. By earthly standards, it was a miracle. If an objective observer met me five years before I became a restaurant owner, my dream would've appeared impossible. It was only through kingdom currency that my dream came true.

In many ways, faith is like a new credit card you receive in the mail. The cards always come with a sticker on the back that says: "Before using, you must call this number to activate." To live life in freedom, we must first dial up God. We must first use our faith to activate the supernatural achievements that take place only in His kingdom.

As a motivational speaker, I go to schools and talk to kids about their dreams. I tell them, "Go to college. College is your ticket to the next level. Education is your ticket to living in freedom." I tell them, in order to find success, they need to get out of the city—clip their wings, cut the umbilical cord, if you will.

But too often, a student will say something like, "My mom says college is too tough. She doesn't want me to go away."

"How does your mom know it's too tough for you?" I ask. "Did she go to college?"

"Well, no."

"Then how does she know?"

The answer is, she doesn't know. I'm sure most mothers who think like that desire the best for their children. But they're not willing to activate their faith. They get the credit card in the mail, but they throw it in the drawer, unused. If they could only dig down and produce a mustard seed of faith, they'd see their dreams for their children fulfilled.

The value of faith doesn't stop after achieving a dream, however. Because, as I've said, success is a journey and not a destination. Sometimes that road is a smooth superhighway; and other times, it's a potholed, gravel back road.

FAITH SUSTAINS US THROUGH GOOD TIMES AND BAD

My dream was to acquire my own *successful* restaurant business. When I received the multimillion-dollar loan from McDonald's, many people thought, "Wow! Kenny's got it made."

But, as I said, that was a *loan*. It was used for the purchase. I had very little left over for working capital, for money to operate the business. I believed customers would come, but I possessed very little knowledge of things like taxes and overhead.

After starting the business, I hit a brick wall. I ran out of cash. Hundreds of thousands of dollars came into my bank account every month, but they went straight back out to cover expenses. I supported 121 employees, and their payroll checks bounced because I ran short on funds. I came home at nights and cried like a baby on my pillow.

Deep in my heart, I believed God wouldn't take me so far just to watch me fail. I believed He brought me to that place for a reason. With a glimmer of faith that everything would work out, I visualized success through my mind's sight and not through my eyesight. Eventually, gradually, the business turned around. Before long, it became the successful business I had envisioned.

Each time I've climbed to the next level in my life, new challenges awaited me. Growing into a new creature is difficult, and sometimes painful. But faith sustains us through good times and bad, through victory and defeat, through death and new life.

The Word says faith makes us whole, and although "the grass withers, the flower fades...the word of our God stands forever."[3] Through His eternal Message, we know nothing can stop the Lord from leading us down the path He's ordained.

(Footnotes)
[1] Mark 9:23
[2] Matthew 13:31
[3] Isaiah 40:8

CHAPTER 3

Acting the Part

A few days ago, I was working through my thoughts on faith for this book when I came across an interview on TBN with the gospel singer, DeWayne Woods. During the 90s, Mr. Woods had contracted HIV. He went through various treatments and spent time in the hospital. He was given no hope, and the doctors told him to get his business in order. He was going to die.

But DeWayne had other ideas. He felt God had given his life a purpose, to sing the gospel of his Lord and Savior Jesus Christ, and specifically to sing about the Lord as a healer. He asked God to heal his body. He meditated on the Word, and then he went about his life. He let go of his problems, gave his health to God, and assumed he'd be healed.

A few years later, he went for a checkup at the same hospital where the doctors originally diagnosed him, and they tested his blood. It came back negative for HIV! The doctors were stunned. They were so baffled; they had DeWayne submit to a battery of tests before a national medical review board. The results still came back negative. The HIV was gone. DeWayne was healed.

Last year, DeWayne released his debut CD. His song, "Let Go," a song about surrendering to God's will and living in freedom, shot up to No. 4 on the gospel charts. As I write this, Woods is on a national tour, spreading God's message of healing and love. He's fulfilling the purpose God has ordained for him.

I BELIEVE GOD WANTS TO DO EXTRAORDINARY THINGS THROUGH ORDINARY PEOPLE

Woods believed God had assigned him a destiny. But he's no different than any of us. We all have a destiny assigned—a destination we're supposed to head toward—and it's our job to believe in it and act like it's already done.

Faith is about expectations. I believe God wants to do extraordinary things through ordinary people like us. But that word *extraordinary* intimidates us, and the only way we'll succeed is to follow DeWayne's advice and "let go and let God"—to keep the faith and not lean on our own understanding. We must act as if God's plans for us are guaranteed to happen.

Recently, I talked with a beautiful young lady who desperately wanted to meet the right person and get married. She was thirty-five and wanted to have a family, but she was distraught because she seemed nowhere close to achieving her dream.

"What's wrong with me?" she asked. "I'm healthy, attractive. I'm nice. I've got a good job. So, why haven't I met the right person? Why is God punishing me?" She had been working the singles scene, she told me, but with no luck.

"He's not punishing you," I said. "He's saving you. There's someone out there God has destined to be your husband. You've got to believe that, and then you've got to act the part."

If God has ordained it, then it's as good as done. "You don't need no singles bars. Or online dating. You just need to believe in God, believe in yourself, and expect that meeting your mate is inevitable."

In the Word, when David was still a boy, he faced the Philistine Goliath with the expectation that God would win the battle for him. He told King Saul that the Lord *"will* deliver me from the hand of this Philistine (emphasis added)."[1] When the king tried to clothe him in his battle armor, David refused. He didn't need the extra help. When David confronted Goliath and the Philistine mocked him, David declared that on "this day the LORD will deliver you into my hand . . . for the battle is the LORD's, and He will give you into our hands."[2]

David believed, without a doubt, that God would take care of him. He believed that his victory was already secured. And, indeed, God delivered a most astonishing victory.

The Detox Program

When we follow God's will and have faith in His plans, we have blessed assurance that—in God's time— those plans are already fulfilled.

But when fear of the unknown overwhelms us,

how do we push out fear and replace it with the faith we need to succeed? The first step is to empty our spirit of the negative influences in our life.

When you were a girl and dreaming of Mr. Right, he was always strong and good, wasn't he? Or when you were a boy and dreaming of scoring the winning shot at the buzzer, the shot always went through, didn't it? Everybody dreams of success, but life gets in the way with its negative influences and drags us down.

WE MUST ELIMINATE THE SOURCES OF DESTRUCTIVE MESSAGES AND REPLACE THEM WITH THE MESSAGE

Think about it. Two of the first words we learn as children are *stop* and *no*. From that point on, the world sends messages that, either intentionally or unintentionally, kill faith and create a vast graveyard of dead dreams.

To give life to our faith, we must eliminate the sources of destructive messages and replace them with *the* Message—the greatest message ever told.

To begin this process, I recommend an intense thirty-day detox program to get rid of negative influences. The first step is to turn off the television. If you want to live in freedom every day, then you can't watch the news. Faith or fear comes from hearing, and what do you hear on the news? Murders. War. Car wrecks. Foreclosures. Economic recession. Natural disasters. You also can't watch all those dramas and sitcoms that focus on violence or make light of immoral behavior. Just turn the television off.

The same thing goes for the newspaper. Cancel it. It carries more of the depressing news, only in further detail. The news industry does not reflect the normal state of affairs. They hunt for dramatic, negative stories. Then they present them together, and we think those problems are everywhere. In reality, it's a highly inaccurate and negative view of life.

All the events in a newspaper have already happened. They're history. You can't do anything about them. I don't read the newspaper, and people ask me how, as a businessman, can I do that? Don't I need the information in a newspaper to succeed?

YOU CAN'T BE WHAT YOU CAN'T SEE, SO YOU NEED TO HANG AROUND PEOPLE WHO WILL SET YOU ON FIRE

The answer is no. Nothing in the newspaper impacts my business. *I* impact my business. My actions impact my business. My faith impacts my business much more than the latest worry screaming across the headlines.

Once you've eliminated the negative influences of the larger world, then you must tackle the tougher job of eliminating the unconstructive influences in your personal world. Namely, negative people. Who are you hanging out with? Who are you spending the most time with? The law of associations says that we become the top five people we surround ourselves with. If those people are naysayers, if they're people who only want to talk about what's bad in the world, if they're people who play the blame game, always assigning fault for their failures at someone else's feet, then you need to detox from them as well.

You can't be what you can't see, so you need to hang around people who will set you on fire, not douse you with cold water. You need to hang around people who will edify you, who are going to tell you that anything's possible.

When you have dreams, you have to protect them. Just like when my wife was pregnant with each of our three sons, she had to live a very careful life to protect them. She couldn't drink. She couldn't socialize with smokers. She couldn't eat unhealthy foods. She had to treat her body as a temple—protecting her baby by guarding what she put into her body, focusing on eating nutritional foods, and drinking lots of water.

Jesus said "unless one is born again, he cannot see the kingdom of God."[3] When we're in the process of being spiritually born again, it's like we're pregnant—pregnant in the faith. Things get into your spirit two ways: through your ear gates and your eye gates. Like my wife, we must guard against what enters our soul—eliminating harmful influences and replacing them with healthy influences. If we don't, our faith will be stillborn and so will our dreams.

Tithing Our Time

Eliminating time-consuming negative influences gives us a gift of time we can redirect toward God. Many church-goers tithe 10 percent of their income, but they barely spend a minute each day with the Lord—probably grace before dinner and that's it. But God wants more than just your money. He wants all of you, especially your time.

He's after a relationship. Intimacy. He cannot be bought off. Just as with our family, we can't develop a healthy relationship without investing time into it.

Jesus says, "Abide in Me, and I in you. As the branch cannot bear fruit of itself, unless it abides in the vine, neither can you, unless you abide in Me."[4] Lest there's any doubt about what He meant by bearing fruit, he reiterates, "If you abide in Me, and My words abide in you, you will ask what you desire, and it shall be done for you."[5]

bowing your head and doing a drive-by prayer at dinnertime.

People don't achieve success through luck or even intelligence, necessarily. One definite key to their success, however, is where they spend their time. They don't major in the minors. They focus on what's most important for their success and minimize the time spent on other things.

WE NEED TO TITHE OUR TIME AS MUCH AS WE TITHE OUR MONEY

To be successful in our faith, we must spend time in prayer and reading His Word. The Word is God-breathed and offers one of the best ways to know Him. When we first read the Bible in earnest, we're a babe in the Word—just scratching the surface of its meaning. But through time, the Word becomes flesh in our lives, and we receive revelation after revelation.

What you read on is what you feed on, and by reading the Word, we immerse ourselves in the Truth with a capital T. Your current challenges might be fact, but they aren't Truth. The Truth contained in the Bible resides in a world where anything is possible—a world where God wields the supreme power to produce any outcome

He wants.

Through the Word, we follow Paul's command to "not be conformed to this world, but be transformed by the renewing of your mind, that you may prove what is that good and acceptable and perfect will of God."[6] Through spending time in Scripture, we are born again into a new abundant life and learn to understand and believe in God's will for that life.

Along with reading the Bible, prayer is the other essential way we spend time with the Lord. The Bible tells us to pray without ceasing. Our prayer time should begin the very moment we get out of bed, beginning with something like, "Lord, guide me today. Let Your will be done. Don't let me get ahead of You."

Rise an hour early and spend quiet time in conversation with the Lord. Find a quiet place—where there's no television, no radio, no snoring spouse—and come into the Lord's presence. For many people, prayer is nothing more than a verbal wish list, but it shouldn't be. Although God does want us to ask for what we need, prayer is much more than a wish list. It's a dialogue. There will be times when you speak, but there will also be times when you keep quiet and listen to the Lord.

Through the years, people who were strong in the faith used to tell me about the Lord talking to them. So, when I made prayer a central part of my life, I was concerned. I didn't hear God's voice. By investing time in my relationship with the Lord, however, I learned that He doesn't speak to most of us in a loud, booming voice with trumpets blaring. He speaks to us like He spoke with Elijah.

When Elijah was waiting on the Lord, "the LORD passed by, and a great and strong wind tore into the mountains and broke the rocks in pieces before the LORD, but the LORD was not in the wind; and after the wind an earthquake, but the LORD was not in the earthquake; and after the earthquake a fire, but the LORD was not in the fire; and after the fire a still small voice."[7]

It was in the quiet whisper that Elijah heard God. And it's there that we too will hear Him. But it takes time and patience to hear God's whisper. It's not something that can be done on the cheap. In order to nurture the relationship and grow in Him, we have to be still and listen.

Prayer and Scripture should be our focus. But in addition, we can read Christian books and listen to gospel music, again serving nutritious food through our eye gates and ear gates.

In Genesis, after God tested Abraham with the near-sacrifice of his son, Isaac, God promised Abraham that "in your seed all the nations of the earth shall be blessed, because you have obeyed My voice."[8] He promised that Abraham's descendants would number the stars and would inherit his blessings.

Through abiding in Christ, we become spiritual descendants of Abraham. "If you are Christ's, then you are Abraham's seed, and heirs according to the promise."[9] Through committing to your faith, by detoxing from harmful influences and replacing them with divine influence, you'll be ready to share in God's promise of living in freedom everyday. You'll be ready to act the part, like DeWayne Woods, and walk in faith—believing the Lord's destiny for you will be fulfilled.

You'll build the required foundation for moving to the next level in your life. You'll be ready to receive your vision of success.

(Footnotes)

[1] 1 Samuel 37;
[2] 1 Samuel 46-47;
[3] John 3:3;
[4] John 15:4;
[5] John 15:7;
[6] Romans
[7] Genesis 22:18
[8] Galatians 3:29

VISION
PART TWO

CHAPTER 4

Envisioning Success

It was a clear, crisp January weekend when I went camping with Bradley and Drake on a Boy Scout outing. Several inches of snow covered the ground from a recent snowfall, and the frozen white blanket glistened beneath the sun.

My middle son, Bradley, was the one in Scouts, but I brought my youngest son, Drake, along too. For one of our activities, the Scout leader took us on a three-mile hike through the snow. Drake wanted to go, too, so I took him. In retrospect, it was a bit much for a five-year-old boy.

We headed out, and Drake did fine at first. It was a strenuous hike; the snow crunched under our feet, and it required lots of energy to step through it and make our way over the many hills.

After we reached the halfway point and turned back, Drake slowed down. He trailed the rest of the crew, and I stayed with him. His energy faded; he quit talking and stumbled a few times.

As we were about to head up a steep hill, Drake grabbed my hand and stopped. "Dad, I can't go anymore. My legs hurt too much." His young eyes pleaded with me as they filled with tears. "I can't move. I'm too tired."

Let me tell you, that's a terrible position for a father to be in. I knew he was exhausted. He'd fought through the first two miles, but now he thought he had nothing left.

"I know you're tired, son," I said. "But you have to keep moving. I can't carry you up this hill and make it through the snow."

He continued grudgingly but quit again after a few minutes. He fell on his knees, sobbing. "I can't, Dad. I just can't."

My heart ached for him, but I knew I couldn't carry him the last mile, most of which was uphill. I had to do something to keep him going. "You've got to dig deep. Just think about when we get back to the campground. We're going to make a bonfire. We're going to roast s'mores. We're going to drink hot chocolate."

With enough encouragement, he got up and again continued walking. I kept painting a vision for him. "Can you see the campfire? Can you see us sitting around it, feeling all warm and telling stories?"

Drake trudged on. Occasionally, a tear fell down his cheek, but he kept walking.

"You're doing great, son. You're getting closer. Keep picturing the campground where we'll sit back and relax."

I kept coaching him, and he kept walking. His eyes stared straight ahead, and I could tell he was using his mind's eye to focus on his destination.

Then we crested the hill, and I spotted our goal. "Look, Drake! Do you see it? Our campground's right down there!"

His face lit up, and he walked faster and faster. The energy returned to him, and he looked like he had never struggled.

We finally arrived. "Wow! I made it!" He was so proud of himself.

The Scout leader patted him on the back and said, "You did great!"

One of the boys came over and said, "I couldn't have done that when I was five. You're a great hiker."

WE NEED TO CARRY A PICTURE IN OUR MIND OF WHERE WE ARE HEADED

Drake beamed. He walked around the campground, walking with the boys and then made some s'mores. The pain in his legs disappeared, and his spirit soared.

Spiritual Sight

That hike was a lot like life. It's often very strenuous. We get exhausted, and we come to a point where we face quitting or marching ever onward. To continue on, we must have a vision. Like Drake, we must picture what success looks like. We need to carry a picture in our mind of where we're headed.

What does success look like to you? Have you crystallized an image of what you want to achieve?

Many people simply tie success to money and declare wealth as their goal. But they don't understand that money is a by-product. It's a consequence of following God's will for your life and living in freedom. It's not a goal unto itself. Money is the fruit of the vision that's inside you; it's what you produce. When you go to the grocery store, you find fruit in the *produce* section. By focusing on money, people fail to develop a proper vision for their lives, so they don't produce the fruits of success. As Helen Keller said: "The greatest tragedy in life is sight without vision."

If we study wealthy people—especially people who didn't earn their wealth, but inherited it—we'll discover that most of them lack joy in their lives. It may be a cliché to say money doesn't buy happiness, but it's true. And what's just as true is that a lack of vision brings pain. The Bible is blunt on this point: "Where there is no vision, the people perish."[1] They might not die in body, but their spirits die. They don't know peace. They don't know spiritual prosperity because they don't operate within God's blueprint for their lives.

Michelangelo once said: "The problem in life is not that we aim too high and miss, but we aim too low and hit it." We hit the low mark because we don't focus. Vision is like a manual focus lens on a camera; we have to zero in on what's ahead. What we focus on the longest is our strongest, so when our field of vision is blurred and scattered, we'll wander through life without hitting the high mark of our dreams.

We can't conjure up a vision on our own, however. We must return to that cornerstone of our success—faith— and spend time with God in order to receive our image of success.

In the book of Habakkuk, the gradual destruction of Judah torments the prophet Habakkuk, and he anticipates its defeat at the hands of the invading Babylonians. He lives in a discouraging world, and he cries out to God, expressing his many concerns and doubts. Although he's distraught, he spends time with God, seeking answers to his problems.

Eventually, God gives him a vision of things to come. He tells Habakkuk to "write the vision and make it plain on tablets, that he may run who reads it. For the vision is yet for an appointed time."[2]

Habakkuk's story tells us several things about vision. The prophet received his vision by waiting on the Lord. Habakkuk communicated with God; spent time with Him. He had a personal relationship with Him. When God gave Habakkuk the vision, the Lord said it was locked in; it was for "an appointed time." The vision was according to God's timetable and nothing could derail it from happening.

BY SPENDING TIME WITH THE LORD, WE DEVELOP OUR VISION

Also, the vision was to be understood and implemented. It wasn't some vague, blurred image, but something concrete. Something that would encourage readers of the vision to run with it—in other words, to give it legs and follow through on it.

We can apply the same lessons from Habakkuk to our lives. By spending time with the Lord, we develop our vision—a vision that is assured under God's timeline and is designed for implementation.

Dr. Myles Monroe said: "Vision is intelligent foresight." It uses faith to develop a spiritual eye, which discerns things that the carnal eye cannot see. Ironically, our carnal sight sometimes blinds us. We allow things our eyes witness to overpower the reality of what we could see through discernment. Spiritual discernment, in fact, is a key to success in every aspect of our lives.

We often hear about businesspeople using vision statements in their companies and business enterprises. Developing those statements is a good thing to do. But when

I coach people, I encourage them to have a vision for all parts of their lives. First, they should develop a vision for their life in general. Then discern their vision for their family. Finally, they should work out a vision for their career and business.

Developing a vision prompts you to ask questions of yourself and your family. What type of person do you want to be? What legacy do you want to leave your family and the world? What kind of family do you want to be? How will you behave as a family? What kind of impact will you have? Those are all questions that point you toward something greater than just your next promotion.

You can't be what you can't see. Without immersing yourself in the Word of God, without listening for that still, small voice of the Holy Spirit, you can't become the person, family member, and worker that God wants you to be. You can't take your dreams off the pillow and make them manifest in your life. You can't experience the freedom that comes from aligning with God's will.

If you invest in your vision, you'll get a taste of success. You'll get that sweet taste in your mouth, and you won't want to return to the darkness of no vision. As our spiritual sight develops, it becomes easier to walk in it—easier to change our habits and our associations. It transforms us into new creatures, and we don't want to return to the old ways that held us captive. It transforms us into a unique masterpiece.

Seeing the Mountain

In the book of Genesis, when the Lord came to Abram and told him to come out of his tent, He told Abram to "look as far as you can see in every direction—north and south, east and west. I am giving all this land, as far as you can see, to you and your descendants as a permanent possession."[3] God showed Abram his destiny—a destiny that was unique to him. Just like Abram, the vision God has for your life is personal. God promised Abram "as far as *you* can see." Each vision is personal, and although you might see it clearly, other people might fail to see it.

Ray Kroc was fifty-two years old when he first saw the hamburger stand operated by the McDonald brothers in San Bernardino, California. He sold Multimixers at the time, and he went to the McDonald's location and saw lines of customers running out the door. He'd never seen a food establishment serve so many customers as quickly as the McDonald brothers did. But he saw more than what other people saw. He saw a concept that could be duplicated in many other locations.

EACH VISION IS PERSONAL, AND ALTHOUGH YOU MIGHT SEE IT CLEARLY, OTHER PEOPLE MIGHT FAIL TO SEE IT

Kroc went to the McDonald brothers and presented the idea of allowing him to franchise their business. But they refused. They didn't possess the same vision he did. They were content to stick with what they were doing and the status quo.

But Kroc caught fire with his vision, and he didn't give up. With persistence, he kept going back to the McDonald brothers and asking to franchise the business. For several years he tried. Eventually, they relented and agreed. The rest is history. McDonald's grew into the world's largest restaurant chain and a gigantic global brand.

Your vision is God's gift to you—given via your faith and your belief that all things are possible. Most people won't see it, so it's important to stand strong against the doubts of others. If you believe your vision is ordained for the appointed time, then your vision *is* reality. It's in the bank.

In Dr. Monroe's book *The Power of Vision*, he tells a story about Walt Disney and a vision he had while at Disney World. One day early in the park's development, Disney sat on a bench in the amusement park and stared into space. A worker manicuring the grounds nearby saw him staring off. He approached him and asked Mr. Disney what he was doing.

VISION IS REALITY. IT IS POWERFUL. IT IS REVELATION. IT IS THE STUFF OF DREAMS

"I'm looking at my mountain," he said, referring to a patch of open ground and open sky.

Of course, the worker didn't see the mountain. But millions of us have seen it since then. The mountain Disney envisioned is the famous roller coaster, Space Mountain. And under Disney's orders, Space Mountain was built.

Unfortunately, Walt Disney died before the roller coaster could be completed. After it was completed, his widow attended the opening ceremony. A Disney official, speaking before Mrs. Disney, celebrated the vision of Walt Disney but also lamented the fact that he didn't live to see his vision.

Mrs. Disney then came to the podium. In her opening comments, she said that she needed to correct the previous statement. "Walt already saw the mountain. It is you who are just now seeing it." She knew the mountain had been real to her husband from the first day he "saw it."

Vision is reality. It is powerful. It is revelation. It is the stuff of dreams. Combined with an enduring faith, it sends us down the road of freedom and out of the arms of slavery.

When we're on life's journey, we must develop and nurture a vision of success, keeping it in focus at all times. The road might be tough. It might deliver steep hills to climb, with sluggish snow to trudge through and bone-chilling temperatures to dishearten us. But we have a destination waiting for us. If we just believe we'll make it there, then God's plan will be accomplished.

(Footnotes)
[1]Proverbs 29:18, King James version
[2]Habakkuk 2:2;
[3]Genesis 13:14-15, New Living Translation

CHAPTER 5

Gifts of a Player

Michele Hoskins used vision to become a player in life. As a young woman, she dreamed of becoming an entrepreneur. Although she worked for various employers over the years, she continued to develop a different image of what life could be like in the future.

Along her road of success, she hit many roadblocks. She tried to interest other people in her entrepreneurial ideas, but no one bought into them. Then, her life took a downturn. She lost her job. She suffered through a divorce and she struggled to pay her bills. Things didn't look good, but still, she clung to her dreams.

During her lowest point, her vision grew even clearer. Michele's great-great-grandmother, a slave named America Washington, had once created a phenomenal recipe for a honey crème syrup. Ms. Washington required her family keep the recipe secret, but she did allow them to pass it down to the third daughter of every generation. Michele was an only child, and her third daughter was slated to inherit the recipe. Michele realized she could leave an even greater inheritance to her daughter than a mere recipe. She could leave her, and her sisters, a business.

The vision was crystal clear, and it empowered her to fight for her dream. To make it a reality, she sold everything she owned and moved back with her mother.

Michele Hoskins made the syrup in her basement and went door-to-door to neighborhood mom-and-pop stores trying to sell her new product. She wouldn't bill them until they sold the syrup, she told them. When the shop owners agreed to take her product on consignment, her family and friends would shop for her syrup at those stores.

Later, she targeted larger Chicago grocers, and after winning them, went after major restaurants and retailers. After calling Denny's every day for more than two years, she won a $3 million contract with the large restaurant chain. Today, Michele Foods, Inc. is a multimillion dollar business, which provides a variety of products to Denny's, Wal-Mart, Albertsons, Kroger, Publix, and Super Target.

Michele shares her inspiring story and her message of hope through motivational speaking and her book, *Sweet Expectations*. She's now spreading the vision to other people who want to follow their own paths of success.

Although Michele Hoskins had no business background, God obviously planted gifts of business savvy and persistence within her. But she had the choice to not follow God's plan. When she was struggling, she could've abandoned hope and spiraled downhill, wandering from job to job. Or she could've bounced back with a secure job, making ends meet while still wondering what her life could've been like. Or better yet, wanting to fulfill some of her entrepreneurial spirit, she could've latched onto someone else's dream and vision, becoming a spectator to someone else's success.

Or she could do exactly what she did go for her own dream and become a player in life.

Make It Happen

A friend and mentor of mine, Herbert Harris, wrote a book titled: *The Twelve Universal Laws of Success*. In the book, Harris identifies four categories of people and their approaches to life.

At the bottom of the list, he identifies the *wanderers*. Wanderers are people who've lost hope—the ability to see past the current day and its seemingly impossible challenges. When people don't remove themselves from a hopeless environment, they lose the energy to play the game of life. They wander from pillar to post, hand to mouth, sometimes working, sometimes not, but usually falling further and further behind. They possess no dreams and no goals.

The next category on the list is the *wonderers*. Wonderers don't play the game of life, either and they're not spectators in the bleachers cheering on the players. They hang out in the parking lot, tailgating, and wondering what's going on. Wonderers hear the cheers, but don't have a clue what they're about.

They watch the news and read the newspaper. They follow other stories and wonder why they can't live their dreams and take their life to the next level. Sometimes, I see wonderers when I go into the barbershop. There, the television plays all day, and I find people watching the TV and talking endlessly about events in far-off places. All they do is talk and talk. They have dreams, and they don't live hopeless lives. But they're stuck.

Spectators sit in the bleachers, cheering the players

on the field. They like being near success, and they internalize other people's success as their own. Once, I was at a restaurant where a large group of men next to me ate and argued about an upcoming Michigan-Michigan State football game.

"We're gonna whoop you guys," one man said.

"Nah, you don't stand a chance," another man said. "You've got no offense. You don't stand a chance against our D."

WHEN PEOPLE DON'T REMOVE THEMSELVES FROM A HOPELESS ENVIRONMENT, THEY LOSE THE ENERGY TO PLAY THE GAME OF LIFE

The debate went on and on with this group, and it got louder and louder. It almost came to fisticuffs. All I could think was, *They keep using "we" and "you" as if they're the ones on the field. But they'll just be watching. They won't be playing the game.*

I did take my sons to a Michigan game recently, and it was an exciting event. The spirits of more than 100,000 screaming fans rose and fell depending on the efforts of the players on the field. In life every day, just like in that game, people attach themselves to the dreams of others. They do it in their careers and in their families. Instead of seeking the peace and joy of living a life in freedom, they pursue happiness through other people.

But a free life isn't a spectator sport. You have to play the game. You have to have a vision, and you have to go out and make it happen.

Players make it happen. They know that God created them as a designer original, and they spend time developing their vision for life. They make plans; they set goals. They take responsibility for their vision, and they don't blame other people when life throws them a few challenges.

It's up to you whether you'll become a player or a spectator, wonderer, or wanderer. It's a choice. You can possess success. It's a birthright. It's available to all of us. At birth, God gives us gifts that make our unique success possible. We must choose to be a player in life and mine the gold that's within us.

In *The Power of Vision*, Dr. Monroe tells the story of a Buddha statue in Thailand. At one time, the government in Thailand wanted to build a highway and the plans called for the road to run through the location of a Buddhist monastery. They had to relocate the monastery, as well as an eleven-foot clay statue of Buddha.

They used a crane to lift sections of the delicate statue and move it to its new location. As they relocated the statue, however, the stress caused pieces of clay to fall off. Onlookers grew anxious for the welfare of the important relic. But as more pieces fell off, workers made an astonishing discovery. Underneath the clay, they found the statue was actually made of gold.

Vastly more valuable than originally thought, today the statue is visited by hundreds of thousands of people. Dr. Monroe uses that story to illustrate how we're "living our lives of clay vessels when in reality we are pure gold inside."

We may work different jobs during our lifetime, but our real job, our real journey, is to discover the gifts that lie buried within each of us. Once we find our gifts, our job is to treat them as precious seeds—nurturing them and ultimately reproducing them.

Believe the Impossible

Your talents are a gift from God, but using them is

your gift back to God. You have to invest time in searching for your gifts, or as I call it, mining your own business.

I have nineteen wonderful employees who are originally from an area in Africa known for its many jewel mines—diamonds, rubies, and such. They talk with pride about the resources lying under the ground of their homeland. But most of the people who live there don't even know what lies inside the earth, and they're certainly not enjoying any wealth associated with that buried treasure. Most of the people from there are very poor, and those who aren't impoverished probably left the country like my employees.

A FREE LIFE ISN'T A SPECTATOR SPORT

We also have precious gifts inside us and don't even know it. We don't mine our own diamond mines. To do that, we must consider what we love to do. We need to look at what we would do if money didn't matter. What would you do if you didn't need the money, but you did it so well, people paid you anyway? In that answer, you'll discover the first clues to your gifts and the first glimmer of light that grows into your vision.

Your vision has to be bigger than the life you're currently living. It has to be bigger than your bank account. Bigger than the expectations people have of you. To most of the world, your vision should seem nearly impossible.

If you struggle with overwhelming challenges, you can't measure them at face value. Likewise, if you pursue your dreams, you can't measure them at face value, either. You have to believe in the impossible.

An Adidas ad that I like states: "Impossible is just a big word thrown around by small men who find it easier to live in the world they've been given than to explore the power they have to change it. Impossible is not a fact, impossible is an opinion. Impossible is not a declaration, impossible is a dare. Impossible is potential, impossible is temporary. Impossible is nothing."

When you change the way you look at things, the things you look at change. You might feel weak and powerless now because you rely on your own strength and worldly expectations, but a vision will empower you. A commitment to a glorious future will give you strength. You'll catch on fire.

YOUR TALENTS ARE A GIFT FROM GOD, BUT USING THEM IS YOUR GIFT BACK TO GOD

Your vision is like a muscle. You have to work it to make it strong. When I first started working out with a personal trainer, I struggled to lift a low weight level. My muscles ached after each workout. But over time, my muscles grew stronger, and I lifted more than I ever imagined when I first began.

Most people don't even visit the "gym" to work out their vision. Most people don't plan to fail; they simply fail to plan. They fail to set goals. They wake up every morning and get in their car and say, "I'm going." But they're going to Destination Nowhere. It's not that they can't have what they want. It's that they don't know what they want. Satan is real, and he is out there, but often the most dangerous enemy we face is ourselves. As T.D. Jakes said, our greatest enemy is not the enemy without, but the "enemy in me."

The pursuit of vision demands courage. Immediate financial circumstances might require you take certain jobs to pay the bills, but through God, you must find the strength to not abandon your passion. Your dreams and your goals should lead you.

Your gifts will make room for you. If you look at people like Oprah Winfrey, Michael Jordan, or Bill Gates, none of them were powerful tycoons when they were children or young adults. They grew into their gifts.

You can't be like the average person who sells out his or her dream for security and a paycheck. That's when we slip, ever so gradually, into slavery. Living in freedom requires that you take a stand and make a commitment. As with Michele Hoskins, it requires that you stare in the face of obstacles and declare "nothing is impossible." It requires that you make a commitment to being a player in life.

THE PURSUIT OF VISION DEMANDS CHANGE

CHAPTER 6

Write it Down

My father, John Brown Jr., had a vision for his five children. Although he made some mistakes early in life, and had his first child when he was a young teenager, he knew what it would take for his children to succeed. It would take education.

Dad pounded into us the need for education. He spoke about it. He wrote about it in letters to us. "Education is empowerment," he said. "Education is the road to freedom."

He viewed education in a holistic way. My four siblings and I must always be learning, he told us. We needed to learn from the Word of God; we needed to learn from the experiences and people around us; and we needed to learn from reading enlightening books. And we absolutely had to learn by applying ourselves in school. His vision for education was so crystal clear. I saw it, too. I didn't go around doubting the value of learning.

Dad had spoken life into us. Not only did all of us graduate from high school, but also from college—all with bachelor's degrees, some with post-graduate degrees. If you've read or heard about my family and my childhood, then you know that was a remarkable achievement.

A God-aligned vision possesses a life of its own, however. It lives and breathes and continues to grow. In order to support his family as a teenager, my father put his dreams on hold. As my siblings and I earned our diplomas, his vision returned to his own long-held desires. "It's time for me to get my degree," he told us, and that's what he went out and did.

A GOD-ALIGNED VISION POSSESSES A LIFE OF ITS OWN

He enrolled in an associate degree program at Pasadena Community College. There, he caught the education bug. He was excited to be in the energy orbit of so many young folks and so much transformational knowledge. On the day he graduated, you would've thought he'd earned a diploma from Harvard. Everyone took pictures of him, and he smiled and laughed and held up his diploma. He was on top of the world.

But he didn't stop there. The vision continued to grow. "Okay, if I can do that," he said, "I'm getting my four-year degree."

And that's exactly what he did. Not long before he died, at the age of fifty-five, John Brown Jr., earned his master's degree. When I think of Dad as a young father in the inner city, and think of the eleven college degrees that he and his children earned, I know anything is possible.

My father's vision made room for him, but he had to give it legs by speaking it and writing it down. To paraphrase the Lord's message to Habakkuk, he had to make it plain so we could run with it.

Keep It in Front of You

My siblings and I could see Dad's vision because he always put it in front of us. But many people don't focus intensely enough on their vision. If your goals are not in front of you, and if you're not referring to them often, then you can't be what you can't see.

Herbert Harris and I conduct a seminar together based on his book, *The Twelve Universal Laws of Success*. After he talks about vision being one of the laws of success, he breaks out a stack of paper and a supply of crayons. He announces to the audience, "Now, it's time for you to draw your vision." He instructs everyone to be as specific as possible; they can use stick figures and crude sketches, but they must use as much detail as possible. He asks them, "In five years, what are you going to be doing? Where will you be living? What will your family look like?"

It's a beautiful process to watch the participants depicting their goals with crayons—having fun and getting in touch with the type of dreaming they did as children. Once they're done, they come up front and share their vision. "In five years, I'm going to be married and have two children." "I'm going to retire from my job." "I'm going to live in the mountains." "I'm going to finally start my own business." "I'm going to live in a new home." "I'm going to travel to the Caribbean."

After they finish their presentation, Herbert has them repeat, "It is already done. It is already done." The thing is, they really believe their vision will happen. They take home their drawing and put in on the refrigerator, or they hang it by their desk. They've tapped into the power of writing their vision and making it plain.

Recently, I coached Paul, a determined businessman who ran a hotel. The business struggled, however, and he told me about wanting his employees to buy into his vision. He kept mentioning the word *vision*, so I asked to see his vision statement. He searched for a copy, but couldn't find one.

YOU MUST CREATE A VISION STATEMENT AND WRITE IT DOWN

I then asked Paul about his training program for new employees. I discovered he'd developed extensive training for the tasks of each position, but he hadn't spent time orienting his employees to the vision statement. The statement wasn't posted anywhere, either, so his employees couldn't internalize it.

"How can your employees buy into your vision if it's not in front of them?" I asked. "It should be written down and prominently placed."

By contrast, I once stayed at a Ritz-Carlton and their commitment to vision impressed me. Their vision statement read: "Ladies and gentlemen serving ladies and gentlemen." Every employee, from the president to the cook to the housekeeper knew the vision, saw the vision, and followed it. When I called the front desk, they greeted me with the warmest professionalism. When I asked a housekeeper for the location of a vending machine, she stopped what she was doing and walked me to it. Each employee embodied the vision.

When you spend time with God, and he gives you a vision for your life—your career, your family, your business—your efforts can't stop with receiving it. You must create a vision statement and write it down. It doesn't have to be long. It doesn't have to use flowery language. It should be plain but it must be written and prominently displayed.

When we record our vision and risk sharing it with others, we make a commitment to ourselves. Too many people walk around with dreams in their heads. They keep them there because they're afraid of the unknown or failure. If you hesitate to write down your vision because you're hedging your bets, then you're committing to *not* following your dreams.

When I speak with many people who desire success and ask to see their vision statement, they can't produce one. When I ask to see their goals, they can't produce those, either. Those are the people who'll take a job for the money and get stuck. They won't take their dreams off the pillow and give them legs. If they had committed to a vision, then everything they did would align with that vision, and they'd make different choices.

Before I opened my restaurant business—before I had the money, before I acquired the buildings—I thought about what I wanted my business to be known for. I developed a vision statement that read: "We will be a role model for what an outstanding restaurant operation should be." That was it—succinct and clear.

As my business materialized, I brought that vision from my head to my heart to my hands. I created a logo and went to Kinko's to make large signs with the logo and the vision statement. I trained every employee in it, and I posted it in my restaurants so my entire staff could see it every day.

The statement didn't mention money. It didn't even mention success, but it guided everyone in our decision making process each day. If an employee's uniform wasn't neat and clean, or if they weren't polite to a customer, I didn't have to pull them into my office and berate them. I could simply walk over and point to the statement and say, "Read the vision."

A CLEAR VISION IS EQUALLY IMPORTANT IN RELATIONSHIPS

In business, and in life, sometimes we talk right but walk left. We say we want to own a business, we want a promotion, or we want a family, but then we do things that don't align with what we want. We must keep our vision visible and in front of us to stay focused.

Align the Goals

I coach people who feel stuck in their jobs—they're not living in freedom when it comes to their careers—and often it's because they're not aligned with their employer's goals. They hire on with the company for the salary, but the company sees a completely different vision than they do. Those people end up failing in business because they're not equally yoked with their employer.

Maybe they want to serve their community through their work when only the bottom-line drives their company. Or maybe they're filled with creativity and ideas, but their company values obedience and discourages varied opinions. Both sets of values may be equally worthy, but if the values aren't aligned, success can't happen.

When I coach people who seek a new job, I tell them the first thing they must ask a prospective employer is to see their vision statement. Forget salary. Forget job description. Before considering anything else, you should look at a statement and be able to say, "Okay, I can latch on to that. That will propel me to my next level."

A clear vision is equally important in relationships. Often, we meet someone, get serious with him or her, and never consider the person's history. Two people meet and experience a physical attraction, but how often do they sit down and ask each other, "Where will you be in five years?" "Are you a believer?" "How are your finances?" "Do you want to get married?" "Do you want children?"

I coached a man, Perry, who struggled in his marriage. When he was growing up, his father worked and his mother stayed home. As an adult, Perry met someone who he found attractive, and he married her because of that attraction. But when they got around to planning for the future, she wanted to climb the corporate ladder. She was a talented woman and had a vision of corporate success. Perry envisioned a large family, with his wife as a stay-at-home mom. The disconnect caused ongoing strife.

When Deidre and I dated in college, we each took out an index card and wrote a vision of where we planned to be five years from then—we listed our priorities and goals. We compared them. Then we walked around for years with those cards—occasionally checking on how we were doing and recalibrating when necessary.

Before we got married, we knew that we each placed God and family first in our lives. We knew we were compatible for the long haul. But Perry and his wife were in trouble. They were headed for a lifetime of resentment if they didn't find a way to develop a new vision together.

Every family should sit down and create a vision statement, including goals that align with that statement. It's hard enough for one person to stay on the correct path, but with two or more people, the odds are even greater of at least one person straying from the family's correct path.

We must take responsibility for our personal vision and for the vision of our family. We can't abandon our dreams to the whims of fate, or assume God will take care of everything without our effort.

God is Spirit, and He dwells within us, but He demands our effort. He uses our hands and feet as tools to accomplish His plans. When a miracle was performed in the Bible, it was performed through a person. God's power makes our achievements possible, but we must take responsibility. If it's going to be you, then it's up to you.

When we lack vision, we don't look any farther than the nose on our face. We amble around each day, wondering what we'll do tomorrow. But with vision, we begin with the end in mind. The ending tells us what steps to take along the way. By default, it creates a plan.

When you build a house, you begin with the end. You create a blueprint that tells you exactly what the house will look like. Then, you work backward and determine each step to take. You see things that might not make sense to people who don't see the plan. You see things clearly.

It's time to build your house. By visualizing and recording your dreams, staying connected to God, and diligently working your plan, you can achieve results as improbable as a poor inner-city teenager producing a family with eleven college degrees. By making choices that align with your vision, you'll be the hands and feet that make God's miracles a reality.

PURPOSE

PART THREE

CHAPTER 7

Place of Assignment

Vision is revelation. It is spiritual sight. It's a movie in your heart that reveals what success looks like for you. Once you tap into your vision, it's your job to enlarge it. You have to use your vision to determine your purpose for every phase of your life.

In ancient Israel, the Lord called the prophet Elijah to serve a specific purpose—namely, to confront the evil that the king, Ahab, and his wife, Jezebel, inflicted upon the kingdom.

Ahab rejected the Lord and instead worshipped the false god Baal, so the Lord gave Elijah an assignment. He sent him to the king with a message: "As the LORD God of Israel lives, before whom I stand, there shall not be dew nor rain these years, except at my word."[1]

The land then succumbed to severe drought and famine, so the Lord sent Elijah to his next place of assignment where God could provide for him. He instructed the prophet to go the "Brook Cherith, which flows into the Jordan. And it will be that you shall drink from the brook, and I have commanded the ravens to feed you there."[2]

Elijah obeyed the Lord, and at the brook, God made a provision for his assignment. Each morning and evening, the ravens brought Elijah bread and meat, and the prophet drank by the water of the brook. But then the brook dried up, and Elijah had to move on to a new place.

Once more, the Lord sent him to a new location: "Arise, go to Zarephath . . . I have commanded a widow there to provide for you." Obediently, Elijah moved on, again. When he arrived, he found the widow preparing to cook her last meal; she was out of flour and oil and was preparing to die. But the Lord provided, and miraculously, the widow didn't run out of food for the remainder of the drought. While there, Elijah brought the widow's son back from death and later went on to defeat the prophets of Baal.

Several hundred years later, God sent an orphan girl on an assignment to save the Jewish people. During the Jewish exile in Persia, the king of Persia banished the queen for acts of disobedience. The king then, improbably, selected Esther, a Jewish orphan, as the next queen.

While Esther was queen, the king's counselor, Haman, conspired to kill all the Jews in Persia. Esther faced risking her life to save her people or remaining silent. When she hesitated to speak up, her cousin, Mordecai asked, "Yet who knows whether you have come to the kingdom for such a time as this?"[3]

Indeed, God had led Esther to the kingdom for such a time. She decided to take a stand. Through defending her people to the king, she saved them from destruction and secured the return of their rights.

I could go on and on, referring to biblical accounts of God sending people on assignment—sending them to a specific place, for a specific time, to fulfill their purpose in life. I could also go on and on, referring to stories of current-day people who are living out their assignments.

Like Elijah and Esther, we are all born with a purpose for our lives. God plants it in us when we are still in our mother's womb. It's an integral part of our DNA. For us to be successful, we have to identify, acknowledge, and honor our purpose. Our assignment is the rent we pay for living in this world.

LIKE ELIJAH AND ESTHER, WE ARE ALL BORN WITH A PURPOSE FOR OUR LIVES

Honor Thy Purpose

We cannot live in freedom if we don't know what our purpose for living is, but we have to move to discover our freedom. When slaves in America sought freedom, they couldn't get it by staying put. They had to escape their current conditions and move to the North. When it comes to living out God's purpose, freedom is a place as much as it's a state of mind.

God takes care of our needs when we live in our purpose. When he calls us to take a certain job, or start a business, or stay home with our children, he guarantees the provisions. With Elijah, God sent the ravens to feed him. Despite the drought, the Lord kept the brook running to provide Elijah water. With us, He provides the financial and spiritual help we need, often through very unexpected sources, so we can work our call.

What God has ordained for us is a promise. He's

mapped out eternity, and He's made us a piece of the puzzle. If we don't understand our piece of the puzzle, then we won't be complete. And the kingdom won't be complete. God will need to find someone else to fill the hole we've left behind.

If you study successful people, you'll find they take time to understand who they are, and what they're supposed to be doing. And they treat what they find as a treasure. They don't say, "Ah, shucks, I can't do that." They honor their purpose by respecting it and following it where it leads. As John D. Rockefeller said: "Singleness of purpose is the one chief essential for success in life no matter what may be one's aim."

God ordered the universe. He put you here for a specific time and purpose. In Ecclesiastes, Solomon said there is a "time for every purpose under heaven." The place God calls you to may be different for different times. He may call you to be a stay-at-home mom during certain years, for example, and then to go into some form of ministry later. Or he might call you to build up your skills in a corporation, and then start your own business after a certain period of time.

The places may change. Like Elijah, our brook at one location might dry up. But the Lord has ordered His plans to stand for eternity. "I know that whatever God does, it shall be forever," said Solomon. "Nothing can be added to it, and nothing taken from it. God does it, that men should fear before Him. That which is has already been, and what is to be has already been . . ."[4] The times and places may change, but God and His plans don't.

When we don't understand the purpose of our life, abuse is imminent. Without purpose, we don't know what we're living for. In the worst case, we get hooked on drugs or alcohol or pornography. In the best case we stumble along, working forty hours a week for forty years to build our 401K. Then, we'll wake up one day in our sixties or seventies and wonder what it all was for.

My friend Reggie remembers when he started focusing on his purpose. It took place on a day when he went out for a business lunch with a client and a few colleagues. During that tense lunch meeting, he happened to glance at the table next to him and spotted a large table of retired folks. They were relaxed, laughing, carrying on, and acting like they didn't have a care in the world. The thought crossed Reggie's mind that many of us, him included, don't plan to truly live life until they retire.

WHEN WE DON'T UNDERSTAND THE PURPOSE OF OUR LIFE, ABUSE IS IMMINENT

Everything Reggie did in his school and professional life, he realized, was geared toward living a joyful retirement. When he was a toddler, his parents put him in a preschool so he'd be ready for elementary school. In elementary school, he was encouraged to work hard so he'd be prepared for middle school, and likewise, in middle school so he'd be ready for high school. He especially worked hard in high school so he could get into a good college. In college, he worked hard in order to get a good job. In his jobs, he worked hard so he could earn promotions and get even better jobs. With each promotion and new job, he tucked more money away for retirement, so one day he could truly have an abundant life. With any luck, he could live a few years in retirement so he could enjoy the fruits of his labors.

What is it all for? he wondered. *Are the last few years the only ones that count?*

After that day, Reggie decided to immediately pursue an abundant life and not wait until the end of his earthly existence. Although it took several more years to discover his purpose, he eventually did. Today, he's a writer and doing what he loves.

The Flow of Life

Reggie had made the mistake that many of us make. We amble along, without clear direction, and we end up identifying ourselves by our job. We identify ourselves by our profession. We go to a party and people ask us what we do, and we say, "I'm an accountant"; or "I'm a teacher"; or "I'm a waitress." We don't say, "I read books"; or "I'm a dad"; or "I'm a servant of Christ."

I know a gentleman who always answers his cell phone by saying, "Hello, this is Bob from XYZ Insurance." Every single time, he answers the phone like that—day or night, business or other. I want to tell him, no, he's just *Bob*; that his identity is through Christ, not through any company or profession.

No matter how many times I give motivational speeches, some people still see me as Ken Brown the McDonald's owner. They're wrong. That's not who I am. I'm Ken Brown the servant leader, the encourager, the family man, the abolitionist.

Without purpose it's easy to get sidetracked along the road of success. Seeking your purpose is the same thing as seeking alignment with God. The Lord has destined a specific path for us, but if we don't pursue it, we can veer off into unintended territory. The place we end up may be drastically different than our place of assignment.

Your purpose is similar to the alignment in your

car. At first, you might not realize your car is inching out of alignment, but as the problem grows, it pulls more and more to one side. The car gets hard to handle. You have to put the car in the shop and have the tires realigned.

When our lives are out of alignment, we're drawn off road. Things get bumpy. Things don't go right. We end up abandoning our assignment and attaching ourselves to other people who are in alignment, who are living in their purpose. We find someone (a business owner, a husband, a pastor) who has the energy—the strut and enthusiasm—and we settle for following their path.

SEEKING YOUR PURPOSE IS THE SAME THING AS SEEKING ALIGNMENT WITH GOD

To get realigned, we have to return to our faith. We have to immerse ourselves in prayer and the Word. We have to spend time with the only One who can correct our direction and set us on the right path.

When we align with our Creator, and do what we're supposed to do, we immerse ourselves into the flow of life. Things tend to work out the way we need them to. If Elijah had panicked, ignored God, and run off to another place, he wouldn't have found the flowing brook or the widow with the endless supply of food. Because he obeyed the Lord, he received what he needed. That doesn't mean things will be easy. Certainly, Elijah faced significant challenges in following the Lord, but in the end, God always provided.

Looking back, I can see how God led me each step of the way to owning a restaurant business. He led me to take a weekend job at a fine dining restaurant. He led a vice president with McDonald's to become one of my regular customers. He led that person, Edie Waddell, to offer me a job with McDonald's and led me to take that job. Later, he led Ms. Waddell to arrange for my purchase of my restaurants. People enter our lives for a reason, a season, or a lifetime, but when we live in purpose, they never enter by accident.

WE ARE BORN WITH AN INNER GUIDANCE SYSTEM —A GPS

The Bible says: "The steps of a good man are ordered by the Lord."[5] We are born with an inner guidance system—a GPS, if you will—that tells us if we're heading toward our destination.

Our destination is out there and if we follow it, things tend to fall in place. Events that seem like coincidences propel us toward our vision. When we're in our kingdom assignment, there are no coincidences.

Along the journey to owning the business, people, resources, and opportunities naturally gravitated toward me. Later, when I felt God call me to a new assignment, more opportunities crossed my path. God led me to speak words of encouragement, write books, and coach others trying to follow their path, and He opened many doors to make that happen.

The world benefits when you follow your purpose. In God's time, your true purpose will ultimately serve God's objectives, namely, to serve His people. In the end, pursuing your purpose in life, going to your place of assignment, is not about you. It's about glorifying God and being a vessel that helps to bring His kingdom to earth.

(Footnotes)
[1]1 Kings 17:1
[2]1 Kings 17:3-4
[3]Esther 4:14
[4]Ecclesiastes 3:14-15
[5]Psalm 37:23

CHAPTER 8

Made By God For God

Don Thompson is the president of Mc-Donald's USA, but it's a job he never expected to hold when he first started out. After graduating from Purdue University with a degree in electrical engineering, Mr. Thompson worked for a government contractor. He didn't look at his profession as his purpose in life, however, and he soon learned that God had something different in mind.

One day, he received a cold call from a recruiter regarding a new job opening. The recruiter explained that the job would involve things like robotics and control circuitry, so as an electrical engineer, it piqued Thompson's interest. When the recruiter mentioned the name of the company, *McDonald's*, Thompson assumed that he meant the aerospace company McDonnell Douglas. At first, Thompson rejected the overture after learning exactly which company was doing the hiring, but he later reconsidered and joined McDonald's.

Thompson excelled in the electrical engineering side of the company, but he eventually realized he'd have to branch out to move up in the corporation. One of his mentors emphasized that McDonald's was an operations-based business and encouraged him to get experience in that area.

Don Thompson eventually left his engineering career to immerse himself in the operations side of the company. At one point, he even worked for six months in a restaurant—flipping burgers and cleaning toilets. There, he discovered a love for working with people and customers, and a love for learning how to run an operation. He was hooked.

Today, after rising rapidly through the company, Don Thompson is the president and he's only in his mid-forties. He's also the company's highest-ranking African-American executive.

Our purpose isn't always what we think it'll be. Sometimes the Lord leads us in a certain direction as preparation for an unexpected future. The Word tells us that Paul, when he was still Saul of Tarsus, trained to be a devout religious expert—someone who would become one of the leading Jewish leaders. But God had something else in mind. He used Paul's background to serve Him and become the greatest Christian evangelist ever. It was a setup for His purpose.

Our past doesn't determine our future, but God can use it as a springboard to doing His work. God used Don's electrical engineering training as an entrée into McDonald's. Now, He's using Don's high profile to show how to live in purpose.

Recently, I attended the National Black McDonald's

Owners Association. While there, I led a devotion service and Bible study program. Don joined the devotion group and even gave his testimony in front of the crowd.

"Everyone who knows me well," he said, "knows the key to my success is I put God first, then my family, and then McDonald's." He said everyone needs to know there's something bigger and better out there driving who you are. "Without a relationship with Jesus Christ," he said, "there can be no success."

The next day, I sat next to Don's assistant during a concert for conference attendees. I asked her if Don's life had changed much since his promotion to president. "It's gotten busier," she said. "But one thing about Don, he always puts God first."

Later, Don Thompson's wife introduced him in front the entire conference. She mentioned many things that she admired in Don, but what she admired most was that when he first started out, then throughout his career, and now as a major executive, his top priority remained devotion to the Lord.

From his position at the top of one of the world's most recognized brands, Don Thompson lives and spreads the Gospel. He acts as a light unto the world. Ultimately, God leads us all to that purpose. He takes us on different paths. He takes us down one direction to get certain experience and then sends us off in another direction. In the end, He intends for us all to serve His kingdom.

Light of the World

As Christians, we talk with other Christians and serve other Christians, trying to make each other happy. But what were Jesus' final instructions to His disciples after He rose from the grave? "Go therefore and make disciples of all the nations,"[1] He said. Spread the Gospel. Lift up people living in darkness.

When we study Jesus' ministry, we notice He didn't spend much time in the synagogues. Where was He? He walked along the byways and highways. He mingled with the people, the lepers and the demon-possessed. He brought good news to the people.

Jesus said, "You are the light of the world. A city that is set on a hill cannot be hidden. Nor do they light a lamp and put it under a basket, but on a lampstand, and it gives light to all who are in the house."[2] Wherever you are along your path, whether you're flipping burgers or running the whole show at McDonald's, your purpose is to be that light.

WHERE THERE IS LIGHT, THE DARKNESS CANNOT EXIST

When we live in our purpose, people notice. "Wait a minute," they say, "there's something different about you." They see the Gospel of Jesus Christ in you; they see the kingdom of God in you.

Where there's light, the darkness cannot exist. When we're filled with purpose, we can enter any dark place and spread the light so others can, in turn, find faith, vision, and purpose. Through embodying the Gospel, we lead people to Christ, and He transforms their lives.

In the earthly world, people will want to look at your past in order to predict your future. When you go for a job interview, you submit a resume, which itemizes every facet of your track record. From that resume, the interviewer looks backward and calculates your future from that historical view. You're in or out based on your past.

Other people meet us in social or work situations, and they judge us based on our current job or title. They don't understand the preparation God has put us through. They pick up the book in the middle, and they can't read the beginning or the ending. They judge based on an incomplete picture.

But God doesn't look at your past to determine your destiny. He already has that figured out.

In the Old Testament, the prophet Jeremiah gets a bit skittish when God calls him to his purpose. The Lord calls to Jeremiah and says, "Before I formed you in the womb I knew you; before you were born I sanctified you; I ordained you a prophet to the nations."[3] That speaks to purpose. The Lord knew Jeremiah before he was even born, and He determined Jeremiah's destiny at that time.

GOD DOESN'T LOOK AT YOUR PAST TO DETERMINE YOUR DESTINY

But Jeremiah doesn't believe he's up to his assignment. "Ah, Lord God!" he says. "Behold, I cannot speak, for I am a youth." The prophet believes his limited past disqualifies him from achieving his purpose.

The Lord responds, "Do not say, 'I am a youth,' For you shall go to all to whom I send you, and whatever I command you, you shall speak. Do not be afraid of their faces, for I am with you to deliver you."[4]

God's message to each of us today is the same. Do you think you're too young? Too old? Too poor? Too uneducated? Then God's message to you is "get over it." Cut out the excuses. Your path is already determined; you just need to hop onboard. In Psalm 139, David, a man after God's own heart, understood the power of destiny and purpose. David sings to God, saying, "O Lord, you have examined my heart and know everything about me. You know when I sit down or stand up. You know my every thought when far away."[5] David understands that nothing is hidden from the Lord. God cannot overestimate our capabilities.

David adds, "You chart the path ahead of me and tell me where to stop and rest."[6] He also understands that his destination is already recorded, and the Lord will accompany him on his journey. "You both precede and follow me. You place your hand of blessing on my head."[7]

David recognizes what the rest of us need to learn. When you follow God's purpose for your life, you can't let circumstances, society, or money determine your net worth. God created us, and we have everything we need for our kingdom assignment. We can't buy into what the world tells us; namely, that we don't have enough education or enough money or enough whatever.

Live Your Making

In Stephen R. Covey's book, *The 7 Habits of Highly Effective People*, he states that highly effective people begin with the end in mind. They look to their destiny and work backward—determining what steps to take based on that destination. For all us, our ultimate destination is to glorify God by serving others.

When we set our sights on fortune and fame, we work toward something that has a shelf life. We work toward something that "moth and rust destroy."[8] We are going to die. It's inevitable. We'll waste our purpose if we aim for fame and fortune. Instead, our true purpose is unavoidably connected to the footprint we leave behind.

How will you perpetuate God's kingdom through your business, job, or family?

My father believed we should live full and die empty. We should give everything we have in us. Everything my father learned and experienced, he put into his children. He deposited his knowledge into me like a seed. I believe when people look at what I've accomplished, they're looking at the fruit of what my father planted. Now I owe the same seeds to my own boys, so they can grow in the wisdom of the Lord and serve His kingdom.

MY FATHER BELIEVED WE SHOULD LIVE FULL AND DIE EMPTY

Riches will not bring us immortality. The names and works of the wealthy and famous may, at best, end up as lines in a textbook or exhibits in a museum. But those who lead a life of significance achieve true immortality by spreading their spirit throughout the universe.

My father always said, "Your life is not for you," and, as a child, I struggled with those words. *What does he mean, my life isn't for me? God gave it to me. It's mine.* But I missed the purpose piece. God gave me this life for a reason, not for a random selection of events, but to work toward a certain goal with a certain purpose. When it comes to our life, either we use it, abuse it, or lose it. When we go through life in a random way, we get stuck on the treadmill, living each day like the last one—just like in the movie, *Groundhog Day*. When we don't approach each day with the end in mind, we abuse the gift of life the Lord gave us.

When you study people who've achieved godly success, who live in freedom everyday, you'll find they've determined that their life wasn't for them. They understood Jesus when He said to become the greatest they had to become a servant. They understood that to use their life, and not abuse it, they had to use their gifts and talents to benefit other people. Through that servanthood, they found the joy, peace, and true prosperity that others have failed to find through fame and fortune.

MAN WAS CREATED, NOT TO MAKE A LIVING BUT INSTEAD TO LIVE HIS MAKING

Man was created, not to make a living but instead, to live his making. In living his making, he will truly make his living. Because He understood the world, Jesus said it's easier for a camel to go through the eye of a needle than a rich man to get into heaven. The world tells us to serve our job, to load up our lives with fancy possessions, to climb the ladder. Then, when we get to the top, we believe the purpose of those below is to serve us— our employees should serve us; our spouse, our children should serve us.

Don't be fooled, man cannot serve two masters. We cannot serve both God and mammon. We must make a choice. We are forced into it.

In Colossians 1:16, Paul says: "All things were created through Him and for Him." Period.

No more; no less. Our ultimate goal is to glorify Him. Our life, our job, our money, our talents, our families, our relationships—they must exalt God. Everything we do is for the sole purpose of His glory. Every person is a unique masterpiece, so every purpose is uniquely crafted. But they all work toward that same goal.

If you're a hotel housekeeper, your job is to glorify God. If you're a minor league baseball player, your job is to glorify God. If you're a young, ambitious president of McDonald's, your job is to glorify God. Insert any job you like, the end purpose is the same.

Your job is to follow the Lord, believe in the impossible, accomplish the impossible, and use your life to spread the light to those still living in darkness. The Lord knows "everything" about you. He "charts the path ahead" of you, and through you, His aims will be achieved.

(Footnotes)
[1]Matthew 28:19
[2]Matthew 5:14-15
[3]Jeremiah 1:5
[4]Jeremiah 1:7-8
[5]Matthew 6:19
[6]Psalm 139:1-2 New Living Translation (NLT)
[7]Psalm 139:3 NLT
[8]Psalm 139:5, NLT

CHAPTER 9

Living for Immortality

We achieve success when we live a balanced life, and when the desires of God penetrate every facet of that life.

Several years ago, I thought I was achieving success. Everything seemed to be going right. My business was getting started, and I was enjoying it. I was managing one hundred and twenty employees and most of them liked working for me. My family was doing well. I was working out with a personal trainer and feeling good. Although I can't say I experienced joy too often, I suppose I was happy.

I didn't realize it at the time, however, but I was stuck in the rat race. I would wake up at 3:30 in the morning and get to one of my restaurants by 4:30. Often, I wouldn't return home until late at night. Some days, I literally worked twenty-four hours. I locked myself in my restaurants—managing the business, putting out fires, and doing my thing.

It was a whirlwind. I had uprooted my family from Chicago and moved them to Detroit. I wanted to be successful, and I wanted my wife to stay home with our three boys. So, I worked my tail off and left my family to take care of themselves.

My first son, Austin, was born while we still lived in Chicago, and I spent some quality time with him during his early years. But my middle son, Bradley, was two when we moved. He got caught up in the whirlwind, and the demands of life strained our relationship.

When I took off a few hours during the weekend, Bradley didn't want to be with me. He didn't seem to miss me whenever I traveled. One day when Bradley was seven, he and I were talking—not arguing, just talking—and he blurted out, "I don't like you very much."

I was floored. *What's wrong with this kid?* I thought he had a problem: *He's detached. He needs counseling.*

The next morning, I spoke to Deidre about Bradley. But she turned the conversation around and made it about me. We'd spoken before about the hours I kept, but I still considered it the right thing to do for my family. I was the provider. I had provided a beautiful home, nice cars, everything we needed.

"You need to stop complaining," I told Deidre. "You have a great quality of life!" I grabbed my cell phone and offered it to her. "Call your friends! Ask any one of them. They would all trade places with you if they could."

But Dee would have none of it. She looked me straight in the eye. "We don't want your presents," she said, emphasizing the "t" sound in *presents*, "We want your *presence*. There's more to life than what you're doing."

Something woke up in me when she said that. My son acted strange because he didn't know me. Dee's agitation had grown because I was never around. Maybe I was happy, but my family wasn't. And no one was experiencing joy. I had to stop and ask myself: *Who are you doing this for? Are you on this wild ride just to serve yourself?*

A Life Examined

Life is an inside job. We don't get out of life what we want, we get out of life who we are. Gandhi said: "You must be the change you wish to see in the world." So, keeping those words in mind, I decided that if I wanted to change my relationship with my family, I had to start first by making an honest inventory of myself. Then I had to make a change.

SUCCESS IS ABOUT LEADING A LIFE OF SIGNIFICANCE AND SERVANTHOOD

Purpose is about balance, wholeness. You can't say you're successful if you don't have a great relationship with your spouse. You can't say you're successful if you don't have a great relationship with your kids, community, church, or co-workers. Success is about leading a life of significance and servanthood.

Living a life of significance is like making a deposit in a bank. You can't go to the bank and make a withdrawal if you haven't made any deposits into the account. With Bradley, I hadn't made any emotional deposits. He didn't know me. The relationship was broken, but once I reassessed my life and spent time with him, the relationship changed. Today, he wants to be around me. When I have to travel, he tells me that he misses me. But I couldn't reap any harvest with my son until I started planting seeds.

My conflict with my family prompted me to reassess my purpose. For many years, I knew my purpose was to build a restaurant business, but now, it seemed my alignment was off. I veered off-road and life got bumpy. I worked too hard, trying to chase earthly success.

Socrates said: "The unexamined life is not worth living," and I set out to take a good look at myself. I sought the services of a life coach, and he prompted me to distribute a 360° survey. A 360° survey is a tool used most often in human resource departments for employees to get a good, holistic assessment of how they perform—their strengths and weaknesses, etc.[1] You take the survey on yourself, and then you distribute it to three types of people—those who report to you, those who work at your level, and those to whom you report. I took the survey myself. I distributed copies to some of my staff, other franchise owners, and my wife (since I report to her) and asked each of them to complete the survey on me.

Each person sent the results separately to an independent company who tallied the results and sent me back a one-page summary. Following the life coach's advice, I also made a list of all the times I felt truly joyful, truly alive. I made a distinction between joy and happiness. I only recorded those moments when I felt completely connected to the Holy Spirit—when I did something that made me feel I was living in total freedom and in total alignment with God.

I love running my business. I love serving my customers. I love serving my employees. But through my examination, I discovered that I truly came alive when I was encouraging others. Specifically, I felt my truest sense of purpose when I stood on a stage with a microphone in my hand, and I spoke to the hearts of the audience—when our eyes met, when the thoughts poured out of me, and when they took feverish notes.

It so happened that the people who completed the 360° profile believed my best quality was not being a business administrator, but was being an encourager and having a vision. God had given me a life story that I could share with others to help lift them up. *I wasn't born to run a business*, I realized, *I was born to be a messenger of hope*. But it also showed that I didn't always succeed at striking a balance in my life. My family, employees, and business associates agreed that I needed to work on maintaining a balance between my professional and personal lives.

YOUR JOB IS TO TAKE PRACTICAL STEPS TO EXAMINE YOURSELF AND DETERMINE YOUR PURPOSE

Like me, your job is to take practical steps to examine yourself and determine your purpose on this earth. For every person God leads to be an encourager, a motivational speaker, or a life coach, there are a million different people with different destinies, different ways to serve others and glorify God. Our job is to make a close assessment of ourselves, ask other people to assess us, and examine those things that bring us joy—those things that make us feel completely alive—and those things that bring us success in all areas of our lives.

Upside-Down Org Chart

In order to fulfill our purpose, we need to understand that each one of us possesses different gifts and talents. In Dr. J. Victor and Catherine B. Eagan's book, *How to Discover Your Purpose in 10 Days*, they say: "There's a greatness on the inside of you. God puts greatness within us as a demonstration of Himself. God is great, and we are made in His likeness and so He made us great. Each one of His creations is unique, equipped, and designed with gifts and attributes necessary to carry out His plans for our lives."

Of course, we're not perfect like God. Far from it. We're so full of sin; it can seem impossible that we have any gifts and talents at all. I've coached people who at first refused to believe they possessed the tiniest portion of greatness. But as the Eagan's said, God puts that greatness in each of us as a demonstration of Himself. What better way to demonstrate His power than to achieve His designs through us.

When people discover their purpose, it embodies everything they do. Henry Ford established the automotive industry, but you can see his purpose in the immense health care system he left in Detroit. Oprah Winfrey built a media empire, but you can see her purpose in the Angel Network that lifts up underserved communities and provides disaster assistance. Truett Cathy founded Chick-fil-A, but you can see his purpose in how he runs his business—including his policy of foregoing millions in revenue by closing on Sundays to honor the Lord's day and provide his employees rest with their families.

I find my purpose in everything I do: in the time and service I give to my family, in the people I speak to and coach. And I find it in my business. If you've ever seen a company's or department's organizational chart, you know that it's a page filled with boxes. At the top of the page you'll find the CEO's or the department head's box. Beneath that are the people who work under him or her—the vice presidents, directors, etc. Below them are boxes that represent people who work under the second level, and so on.

However, when I created a recent organizational chart for my business, I flipped it. I put myself at the bottom with arrows pointing up to my supervisors, and then arrows pointing from them to our line managers, and then from them to our front line employees. My employees don't serve me, but I serve them. They, in turn, serve our customers.

Business motivator T. Harv Eker said: "How we do something is how we do everything." So, how you love God is how you're going to love His people. How you're willing to acknowledge and honor the gifts He gave you is how you're going to live out your purpose.

I CANNOT EMPHASIZE ENOUGH THAT THE PURSUIT OF WEALTH IS NOT YOUR PURPOSE

As I've mentioned before, money will follow you when you focus on your purpose, and serving my employees is just one example of how that happens. By serving my employees, they enjoy their job and want to perform well. And by performing well, our customers are happy and will keep coming back and spending their money with us instead of another restaurant.

I cannot emphasize enough that the pursuit of wealth is not your purpose. In his book, *Your Road Map for Success*, John Maxwell gives an example of a small group of the world's wealthiest men who met in Chicago in 1923. At the time, the men controlled more wealth than the entire U.S. Treasury. How did their lives end up? Did they feel fulfilled? Did they have joy?

Maxwell gives us the details:

"Charles Schwab, president of the largest independent steel company, died broke. Arthur Cutten, greatest of wheat speculators, died abroad insolvent. Richard Witney, president of the New York Stock Exchange, died after being released from a Sing Sing prison. Albert Fall, member of the U.S. President's cabinet, was pardoned from prison so that he could die at home. Jess Livermore, the greatest bear on Wall Street, committed suicide. Leon Fraser, president of Bank of International Settlements, committed suicide. And Ivar Kreuger, head of the world's greatest monopoly, committed suicide."

Wealth did not, in any way, give the country's wealthiest people what they needed. They died leaving their purpose behind—and their money.

Instead, when you give the money you make to your purpose, people's lives are changed. For example, as a servant leader, I felt God calling me to offer health insurance to my staff. That's something most people in my position don't offer. As we all know, health insurance is incredibly expensive. At first I offered to pick up 30 percent of the cost of premiums, but nobody took me up on it. It was too expensive. Then I offered to split the premiums 50/50, but only one person signed up. After she saw how much was deducted from her check, she backed out of the program.

Then one morning while in the shower, I heard God's whisper; I felt His gentle nudging. "Provide. Provide," He seemed to say. From that point on, I knew I had to offer 100 percent coverage. I bit the bullet and somehow made it work.

About two months later, I left one of my restaurants at night and was halfway home when I received a phone call. My manager had just collapsed with a heart attack in the washroom. The ambulance was on the way. She was rushed to the hospital and, thankfully, survived.

Not only did I receive a scare regarding an employee and someone I cared for, I also received a wake-up call. I understood why I needed to provide the insurance. Imagine if I'd been disobedient; if I had chosen profit over people. It could've been catastrophic for my manager. Instead, she continued to receive excellent health care throughout her surgery and recovery. Without the coverage that God directed me to provide, she might not have recovered. Or she might not have recovered enough to continue working. Medical bills would have piled up as her income disappeared. And less important, but not insignificant, I would have lost a critical member of my team.

The wealthy men identified in Maxwell's book died broken, but people who achieve "wealth of purpose" go to their heavenly reward completely whole and completely fulfilled.

In the last chapter, I explained how my father spent his entire life instilling wisdom in his children. After he earned his degrees, he became a teacher and continued to lift up the young minds he educated. My father died three years ago, and I spoke at his funeral. I carried with me an infinite love and deep admiration for my father, but at the funeral, I found I couldn't cry. I realized he'd lived a complete life; his purpose had been fulfilled. My father's life will outlive him and has outlived him.

Since that day when I committed myself to serving others, I intend to use up my life as well—to live an abundant and free life, a life of significance. If I stay tuned to God and follow the purpose He's laid before me, then like my father, my life will continue on as well.

(Footnotes)

[1] The Franklin Covey Company is one such organization that offers 360° profile services.

PASSION

PART FOUR

CHAPTER 10
Plugging into the Energy

Paul received his purpose when he traveled along the road to Damascus. Christ came to him in that blinding light and gave Paul the meaning of his life—to spread the Good News. With his purpose in hand, Paul passionately took to his task. Two thousand years later, we can read his letters and feel his enthusiasm—his zeal for saving the souls of those who would listen. He traveled from city to city; he endured shipwreck; he suffered beatings, but nothing could stop him from his purpose. His passion propelled him.

Paul possessed a thirst that could only be satiated by following God's plan. No prison shackles or hazardous travel could stop him from pursuing his passion. Christ was in him, and He gave Paul joy regardless of the circumstances.

Most of us aren't fortunate enough to receive a message from Jesus as obvious and unforgettable as Paul's Damascus Road experience. Instead, we must pay attention to His whispers and nudgings. But when we pay attention, when we honor our vision and purpose, something comes alive within us.

We are like Mary's cousin, Elizabeth, when she welcomed the pregnant Mary to her home. Inside the womb, Elizabeth's baby, John, leaped at the sound of Mary's voice. And Elizabeth was filled with the Holy Spirit. Purpose leads to passion; when we follow our purpose, joy leaps inside of us and a spiritual passion takes over.

WHEN WE HONOR OUR VISION AND PURPOSE, SOMETHING COMES ALIVE WITHIN US

Success requires passion. It requires a boundless enthusiasm that cannot be shackled; that cannot be enslaved. Passion is spontaneous combustion. We set ourselves on fire, and through that fire, we experience the joy of freedom.

If you love what you do in your life, then you'll never work another day in your life. When you do something with all your might, when you put your whole soul into it, when you stamp your activities with your deepest personality, you're on your way to success. With the activity, energy, and faith that come through passion, you can accomplish far greater objectives than the person who sleepwalks through life. Ralph Waldo Emerson said: "Nothing great was ever achieved without enthusiasm."

The word *enthusiasm* comes from the Greek word *enthousiasmos*, which means to be filled with God. With faith, vision, and purpose, we don't need to seek fulfillment through outside sources. We don't need to attach ourselves to someone else who is living out his or her passion. We don't need alcohol or drugs. We don't need anything that someone can give us or we can buy. We discover our fulfillment, the joy we seek, through Christ who is in us and the passion He gives us to live an abundant life.

Like most people, I used to wake up every morning to the annoying sounds of my alarm clock. But today I don't need a blaring buzzer to get me up. I'm ready to go. I don't need a clock because my clock is inside of me. My burning desire for the path I follow gives me energy. When I leave my house in the morning, I don't go to work, I go to life and get paid for it. I don't need caffeine. I don't need vitamins or an energy drink. The Holy Spirit has already given me the energy I need.

I GO TO LIFE AND GET PAID FOR IT

Most people live for the weekend. But what a waste of life it is to wish away 70 percent of our time here on earth. My weeks don't end. When I'm living passionately, every day brings me energy and excitement.

People see that energy in me and they ask, "How do you do it? How do you have so much spark and fire?" They ask me that, thinking I'll provide them with some medical or diet or exercise answer, but all I can offer is a spiritual answer. I've dug deep, uncovered my passion, and tapped into it. My answer disappoints some people because they want a quick fix, an easy way out of the doldrums.

The World Needs People Who Come Alive

I've heard reports that more than two-thirds of American workers dislike their job or their profession. That's why declining productivity is a problem in many industries. That's why absenteeism and tardiness are problems as well. People don't enjoy what they're doing, so their energy and enthusiasm suffer. They live a mundane existence because they're not filled with God. They have no *enthousiasmos*. They don't follow God. They put their paycheck ahead of their passion.

It's obvious when someone hasn't tapped into his or her passion. When I coach them, I ask, "What's your dream? What are your goals?" They seem to have them, but they can't articulate them. Those people are sluggish, with an "ah-shucks" attitude toward life.

"How can I get excited about your dreams if you're not even excited about them?" I respond. I tell them they'll have to discover their passion and pursue it with a boundless zeal before they can take practical steps toward success.

People who are passionate about life can't wait to get up in the morning. They open their eyes, and their thoughts are spinning; they're anxious to embrace the opportunities that the day has for them. They love what they do, and they do what they love, and success seems to be a certainty for them. And they know it.

Passion is an effortless tide of supernatural power. Most people look to others for the spark they need. They're like all those businesspeople in an airport desperately searching for an electrical outlet to plug their laptop into; they look for someone who has energy to spare, so they can plug into it. With passion, however, you have your own limitless battery.

The spiritual nature of passion offers an eternal flame that can only be extinguished if we let it. The gifts inside us unleash a fire, which will burn as long as we tap into those gifts.

People will pay to watch you burn. Think about it. When you go to a sports or an entertainment event, you pay to watch people who are passionate about what they do. Whether they're actors on a stage or players on a field, they live for what they do. They step on the stage and burn, and we stand in line and pay to see it happen. But in those rare times they don't act with passion, everybody knows it. During a sports event, in particular, the fans boo the players unmercifully.

When we're on the stage of life and don't give it our all, people notice. They might not boo us to our face, but they won't promote us, they won't give us the job, they won't give us the contract. We get stuck and seek other people who do what we won't. We live vicariously through those people.

On any Saturday, go to a Little League game or a kids' soccer game, and you'll spot plenty of parents who live vicariously through their children. They yell at the officials, or they rage at their kid because he or she doesn't live up to the parent's need to feel some passion. You see the same people reading *Star Magazine* and devouring every irrelevant tidbit of gossip about the latest hot celebrities. Or you see them at a restaurant, like the men I mentioned in Chapter 6 who talked and argued about the latest game, using phrases like *"we* beat *you."* That's why stars and athletes earn so much money.   There are millions of paying customers living vicariously through their passion.

Harold Whitman said: "Don't ask yourself what

the world needs, ask yourself what I can do to come alive. Because what the world needs is people who come alive." When you truly come alive, you're sold out; you're unavailable to the obstacles that drag down other people. When someone tries to buy a ticket for a sold-out concert, they're out of luck. When the enemy tries to attack you, he'll find there's no room in your life for nonsense or drama. You're sold out to freedom. You're too focused on your passion.

YOUR DESIRE FOR SUCCESS MUST OUTWEIGH YOUR DESPAIR

I would rather work with one person with passion than ten people without it, because passion gets you through the tough times. When you look at people who race in triathlons—they're running, biking, and then swimming—something has to get them through all the challenges to the finish line. They must possess an enthusiasm they can channel into incredible feats of success.

When challenges confront you, your desire for success must outweigh your despair. Roadblocks are put in our path to test who really wants to arrive at their destination. Those who want it badly enough will apply their enthusiasm to get around the roadblock, but others who succumb to despair will also succumb to the obstacle.

The Lord never promises things will be easy. When we recall Paul's passion for spreading the Gospel, we have to also remember that five times he was whipped, three times he was beaten with rods, once he was stoned, and three times he was shipwrecked. In his constant journeys, he was "in perils of waters, in perils of robbers, in perils of my own countrymen, in perils of the Gentiles, in perils in the city, in perils in the wilderness, in perils in the sea, in perils among false brethren."[1]

Passion not only gives us energy when things go our way, but it gives us energy when everything goes against us. In Hebrews, it says: "Let us lay aside every weight, and the sin which so easily ensnares us, and let us run with endurance the race that is set before us."[2]

Fighting the Good Fight

I was at the airport recently trying to board a flight home. Weather had delayed the flight, and I went to the counter to get some help. The attendant there didn't even look up at me when I approached. She answered in a monotone yes or no to every question I asked. She typed away on her keyboard, checking out my options, but she put no energy into her efforts; she was indifferent to my needs.

While I waited for her, I happened to look at her name tag, which was pinned to her lapel. Her name was Cassandra, and below her name was her photograph. *Wow*, I thought, *that's a totally different person*. In the photo, Cassandra stood up straight with a huge smile. Her eyes sparkled. She looked like she was on top of the world.

Her employer probably took the photo on her first day on the job. Her expression said, "I got it! I made it!" I'm guessing she'd chased such a job for a while, and on that day, she was thrilled. But since then, obstacles had entered her path. Her desire had disappeared. Challenges had beaten her down. It was just a job now.

When people don't live with passion, it's a lose-lose proposition. They live with unhappiness and do sub-standard work, and consequently make their employer or customer unhappy as well. All parties suffer. The same thing goes for passion in a relationship. When people just go through the paces, when they don't approach their relationships with enthusiasm, everyone suffers. No one is happy. Obstacles will enter into your relationships, and you'll have to rely on your passion to keep those relationships growing.

When you're against the ropes, and it seems like the world is against you, your only option will be to reach within yourself. You cannot depend on the passion of others to keep you on your personalized road of success.

WE MUST FIGHT FOR OUR PASSION

Recently, I watched an episode of *The Contender*, a reality TV series that follows a group of boxers through their elimination-style competition. In this episode, I watched as a boxer was getting beaten to a pulp. His opponent took a huge swing at him, and somehow he summoned the energy to duck the blow. After the miss, the guy receiving the blows took on new life. He threw a punch, and it connected, and then he connected with another. He was like a combustion engine, landing blow after blow—rapid fire—until he finally prevailed and won the bout.

We must fight for our passion. We must fight back against obstacles. We must fight for it as if our very lives depend on it. In fact, our spiritual lives do depend on it. When I'm doing seminars with Herbert Harris, he tells the story of two men—one who was successful in life and another who wanted to learn the secret to success.

The man wanting to learn kept inquiring about how to succeed, and finally, in response, the successful man took the man to a lake. They walked into the water, and the first man told the second to put his head underwater. The first man then grabbed the second's head and held it under. He held it under much longer than was comfortable, but eventually he let the man come up. When he did, the man came up gasping for air, sucking in as much as his lungs could possibly hold.

"Why did you do that?" the man asked incredulously after his breathing finally calmed down.

"The way you felt when you came up," the other man said, "every breath you took was like a breath of life. That's what you have to feel when you deal with your dreams. You have to want it like your life depends on it."

Living in freedom depends on living in passion. In order to escape those things that hold us in bondage, in slavery to a nowhere life, we must treat our dreams with energy and enthusiasm. We must never give up.

(Footnotes)
[1] 2 Corinthians 11:25-26
[2] Hebrews 12:1

CHAPTER 11
Fishing and Cooking
and Loving What We Do

While in college, I became good friends with a fraternity brother of mine, Stephan Franklin. Stephan has always been passionate about life, and he's never let the events of life take over his dreams.

He loved the college experience while we were at Southern Illinois University, Carbondale—in particular, he liked the lifestyle and the campus environment. Because of that love, he became an RA, a Resident Assistant, and assisted young students through their time on campus.

After earning his master's degree, Stephan considered his passions in life before determining his next steps. He knew two things: he enjoyed guiding students through their college careers, and he loved being near the water—going fishing, eating seafood, and enjoying the warm sea air. Following his passions, he sent resumes to colleges along the West Coast, and landed a job as Resident Director at the University of California in Santa Barbara. He pursued freedom and found a job, and a location, that brought him joy. Today, he is Assistant Dean of Students.

After moving to California, he also followed his other love, fishing, on the weekends. He would charter large fishing boats and then recruit twenty to thirty of his buddies to join him, covering his costs. He would then get to fish for free.

On board, he'd cook up some of what was caught, impressing everyone with his culinary skills. He created his own marinades. He grilled mahi-mahi, trout tips, and tuna. He grilled vegetables to perfection. Watching him, you could see how excited he was to prepare delicious food and to have so many people enjoy it. In addition to campus life and fishing, he had discovered another passion.

One day, Stephan called me for some business coaching. "I love cooking, and I want to turn it into a business."

I gave him some pointers, which he used to move forward with his dream. He gave his fledgling business a name, *Simply Marvelous Barbeque*. He took out a small sum from savings and registered the business, created a logo, and ordered T-shirts.

He started out selling his services to people he knew. He told colleagues and friends that if they hired him for a job, he would offer the food at cost and donate his services. At that time, Stephan wasn't interested in the money. He had a good paying job at the college. He just wanted to break even so he could follow his passion to the next level.

Gradually, he marketed the business and made

a name for himself. He catered small parties and then moved up to weddings. He earned a small profit and re-invested it into nice equipment—chafing dishes, serving utensils, tablecloths—the whole nine yards. The spreads were beautiful.

Today, two years later, his business is thriving. Stephan and I were in Chicago recently, and while we were together, he kept receiving phone calls from people interested in hiring him and faxes from people signing and returning contracts.

ENERGY, ENTHUSIASM, AND CREATIVITY ARE ALWAYS NEEDED TO MAKE MONEY

Stephan has always followed his heart. He knows what gives him joy, and he uses that joy to guide him. He doesn't chase after wealth or success. Money and accomplishments come to him through his enthusiasm. He found his treasure where his heart was.

Guided by Passion

Conventional wisdom says it takes money to make money—meaning you must invest money up front in order to make more money in the long run. But that statement isn't completely true. Sometimes money is needed in order to earn money. Sometimes. But energy, enthusiasm, and creativity are always needed to make money. Passion attracts it like a magnet.

In *From Welfare to Faring Well*, I wrote about how, on a fluke, I took a job at Lorenzo's Restaurant. I didn't need the money, but I did need to follow my passion for one day running my own restaurant. While I worked there, I had no idea how much money I earned. I'd walk around with paychecks in my pocket and eventually hand them over to Deidre to be deposited.

However, I did know how much I liked working in the restaurant environment. I loved it. And it showed. It showed to my customers. In particular, it showed to one of my regular customers who just happened to be a major executive at McDonald's. And one thing led to another.

Today, I've discovered that same passion for public speaking. Some people have told me, "Ken, you talk too much. Sometimes, you just need to shut up and listen." But, oh, how I love to talk. Now that I've developed a career in public speaking, I'll speak anywhere, anytime. I'll speak for free. I don't care about the money, because I know the more I speak, the more money seems to come to me. Maybe I do talk too much, but now I'm getting paid for talking. I can't beat that.

It's doing what you love that's important. I grew up in Chicago and enjoyed watching Michael Jordan play with the Bulls. At first he caused some consternation with Bulls' management because he wanted to play basketball anytime and anywhere he wanted. The standard NBA contract didn't allow for that. Management was understandably concerned about their investment in Jordan. They paid him a lot of money, and they didn't want him messing things up by getting injured in an unimportant pickup game. But Jordan explained to them that he didn't play basketball for wealth; he played for the love of the game. It wasn't for the money that Michael Jordan became passionate. It was for his passion that Michael Jordan earned so much money.

Often people I coach tell me, "I want to be successful," but with some of them, I know they lack a deep desire.

For one thing, people who are destined for achievement don't say "I want to," they say, "I'm going to." They know it will happen. They know because the burning fire inside won't consider failure as an option. No matter how many hours it takes, or how many years it takes, their enthusiasm leads them to realize their dream. Passion translates into commitment; commitment translates into persistence; and persistence translates into success.

Working in the service industry, I get a close-up view of how well the industry is doing. I believe service in this country is at an all-time low. It's not because of global competition, or because jobs are migrating overseas; it's because people aren't passionate about service. People aren't passionate about excellence. Many people in the industry, possibly a majority, are like Cassandra, the ticket agent from the previous chapter. They're not in it for the love of the game; they're in it for the money. Unfortunately, they find that there's not enough money in the world to make up for a lack of passion.

THERE IS NOT ENOUGH MONEY IN THE WORLD TO MAKE UP FOR A LACK OF PASSION

Renell, a woman I once coached, wanted to go into business for herself. She said she wanted to own a day care center. That got my attention because she'd never had any children of her own, and she didn't have any experience working with children.

"Do you have a passion for working with children?" I asked.

"I guess," Renell said. "Actually, I'm looking at it more from a business opportunity. It's a good market for day care centers, and I think I can make some good money."

It was clear she didn't have a passion for going in that direction. I had to be honest with her and told her that I didn't think she'd succeed. In fact, she might lose money. Renell didn't have the required passionate desire, and she was doing it for the wrong reasons. "What work gets you excited?" I asked. "That's where you should start."

Po Bronson, author of *What Should I Do with My Life?*, says that "most people have good instincts about where they belong but make poor choices and waste productive years on the wrong work." A major problem with making those poor choices is they arrive at the end of their life and wonder what it was all for. What was the purpose of their life? Why were they here? They're filled with regrets.

I heard once of a study where people in their eighties were asked if they had any major regrets over the way their life had unfolded. More than 90 percent of the respondents said yes, they did have major regrets. They had regrets because of the poor choices they'd made. They had regrets because they'd never learned to live in freedom.

We get destination disease. We get some great job. Or we marry a perfect woman. Then we stop and consider ourselves successful. That's when the trap is set. I don't believe you can be entirely successful until the day you die. On that day, if you can look back and see you've pursued your vision with passion, then, and only then, can you say you're successful.

Life requires us to periodically reassess where we are and make adjustments. Sometimes you have to ask yourself: *Am I living this thing called life or is life living me?* That's where the five-year plan is so important. At least once a year, you must look ahead and assess where your passion wants to go. Then, you must determine if you're headed in the right direction. You'll end up somewhere in five years, but will you get there by accident or on purpose?

A Giver Not a Taker

At one point during my restaurant career, I made some poor choices and ended up without a job. To make ends meet, I took a job I didn't want as a Wendy's restaurant manager. It was a great business and the owner was an excellent employer. But I had worked as a Wendy's manager before in my career, and it seemed like a step backward. I was drifting.

I didn't get excited going to work each day. I felt groggy in the morning. My heart wasn't into the job. My pas-

WHEN YOU ARE NOT PASSIONATE, YOU BECOME A TAKER NOT A GIVER

sion was dying, and I was becoming like that airline ticket agent. I realized I was dying spiritually, and I went back and referred to my five-year plan. I developed a strategy to get back on track.

That was a critical time for me. I could've allowed my performance to spiral downward and become a cancer in the company. Instead, I made a plan to find my passion again and to come alive again.

Because I lacked passion at the Wendy's job, I worked just like any other person– an average employee. I didn't leave a footprint, a legacy. I didn't leave anything. I simply went there and didn't give anything. I was a taker—doing the minimum and taking my pay. They probably don't even remember me.

When you're not passionate, you become a taker not a giver. We witness that all the time with people in their relationships. When they don't care passionately about their spouse, children, or friends, they focus on themselves. They focus on what they can get from the relationship instead of what they can give to it. They don't lead a life of significance because their focus is out of whack.

Instead, we can recognize a passionate focus in someone like Dana Reeve, the wife of actor Christopher Reeve. When an equestrian accident tragically paralyzed Mr. Reeve, his wife's dedication to him amazed everyone. She was his true partner, standing by him at public events and assisting him in his intensive care. She helped form a foundation dedicated to researching new treatments for spinal cord injuries and improving the quality of life for paralysis sufferers. For Mrs. Reeve, the passion she felt was not for her husband's money or fame, but for the man himself. Because of that, she gave to him in ways that impressed the world.

In our personal relationships, we must act with passion. But in our working lives, sometimes we have to strike a balance between following our passion and paying the bills. When I coach someone, I never recommend they quit their job and follow their dream without considering the immediate consequences. When you have a spouse or children to support, for example, you have to balance your passion for them—your need to take care of them—with your passion for your work.

That being said, you must always find ways to feed that passion. When I discussed vision, I wrote about a camping trip and a hike I took with two of my sons. The trip was during the winter, and after our hike, we built a campfire. The fire kept us warm for a while, but it began to die. One of the Scout leaders came over and started adding logs to the fire. "You have to keep feeding the flame," he said, "or it will burn out."

We can say the same thing about our passions. If we don't find some way to feed them, the flame will go out. My friend, Stephan Franklin, is a good example. He didn't quit his day job, but he started out cooking for friends on fishing charters, and then gradually, he built a catering business doing jobs on the weekends.

YOU HAVE TO KEEP FEEDING THE FLAME

You may only have ten hours a week available at first, but you must stick with it. Your life of freedom depends on it.

The life of Jesus offers the best example of someone living a life of passion. His passion for us—His love for His followers, both then and in the infinite years to come—drove His life. His enthusiasm for His people continued through His greatest passion— the passion on the Cross.

Jesus is the model we have to follow. He dedicated His life to His love. He gave His life to His love. The least we can do is follow our passion. We insult our Savior by assuming we have limits, by assuming we must sell out for a paycheck. He went to the Cross so we could live in freedom and have abundant life. It's our job to make sure we act on the life He intended for us.

CHAPTER 12

Working the Success Attitude

I n August 2005, Hurricane Katrina pounded the Gulf Coast and left behind the most destructive disaster in our country's history. The three levees around New Orleans couldn't contain the flow of water and gave way, flooding most of the city.

My grandmother, and some of my distant family members, who lived in New Orleans had to flee. They joined the thousands of evacuees who reestablished themselves in new cities.

Soon after the disaster, I was asked to speak to a group of evacuees. I offered them my empathy and as much comfort as I could provide, but I also told them their attitude would determine how well they would overcome the situation. "Life is 10 percent what happens to you and 90 percent how you choose to respond." I shared my personal story with them, including all the evictions I experienced as a child. "Now you've been evicted. But I overcame it and so can you."

I reassured my relations, and my immediate family in Chicago encouraged them to resettle permanently there. A few of them did resettle in other cities like Houston, but to my surprise and disappointment, most of them wanted to return to Louisiana.

In New Orleans, they had lived in the projects. Poverty surrounded them, but now they had a chance to make a fresh start. It was a time to make lemonade out of lemons. An abundance of services and financial assistance were available to help them make that new start. Other than the trauma they still dealt with, it was a golden opportunity. But they wouldn't take it.

ATTITUDE IS MORE IMPORTANT THAN YOUR PAST

They returned to the comfort of the devil they knew. They didn't have a passion for life. They didn't have a desire to step up to the next level. Their lack of passion shaped their attitude, and their attitude shaped their outcome. They returned to being stuck. They returned to poverty.

Passion fosters in us the attitude we need to succeed. Passion is the parent and attitude is the child, but without the child, success isn't possible. When we're stuck in a dead-end job, we might struggle to maintain the best attitude. We know we should be positive. We know we should be determined, committed, but we lack the fire in the belly for what we do, and our attitude succumbs to negative thoughts and a ho-hum approach.

Attitude is more important than your past. It's more

important than your skills. It's more important than your level of income or education. Often, we can't change any of those things. Certainly, our past is set in stone. It's over with. And our boss determines our income. But we have total control over our attitude. By developing a powerful attitude, we impact our achievements far more than any of those other things can.

Setting the Temperature

Events plus attitude equals outcome. Your attitude toward success, freedom, and relationships—and your attitude toward your health, wealth, and joy—these determine how your life will turn out.

WE MUST LIVE OUR LIVES AS A THERMOSTAT, NOT A THERMOMETER

Attitude determines your altitude. Unfortunately, most people I come across don't possess a success attitude. They don't believe they can do it, or they don't think they deserve it. Consequently, they fail. I'm not talking about being arrogant or believing you're perfect, but I am talking about having that deep confidence in yourself—that deep confidence which believes freedom is a birthright and that God will make your vision a reality.

Since life is 10 percent what happens and 90 percent how you respond, if you simply let events batter you around, then you only live 10 percent of your life. The only way people don't succeed is by not believing they can. The only way to move that number up from ten to one hundred is to live your passion and shape your attitude.

We must live our lives as a thermostat, not a thermometer. You put a thermometer in a room or an oven and the temperature reading changes to match its environment. It fluctuates up or down depending on the situation.

But a thermostat *sets* the temperature. Last night, my room got a bit cold, so I set the temperature to 70 degrees, and the temperature went up. My thermostat improved my situation. We have to do the same thing with our life and environment. We can't act like a thermometer; when the going gets bad, we can't go bad. Instead, we must determine where we want to be and make the necessary adjustments—have the necessary attitude—to make that setting a reality.

There will be times when life isn't right, when the temperature of our environment is out of whack, when obstacles block our path. But stumbling blocks are only stepping-stones, and obstacles, as with Hurricane Katrina, are doorways to new opportunities.

Rev. Robert Schuller said: "Tough times never last, but tough people do." We *are* going to experience tough times—that's part of the definition of life. Things aren't going to work out the way you thought they would. People will scoff at your ideas and dreams, but that simply doesn't matter.

Thomas Edison, this country's all-time great inventor, knew a lot about stumbling blocks, but he believed those obstacles actually highlighted his path to success. "I didn't fail ten thousand times," he said. "I successfully eliminated, ten thousand times, materials and combinations which wouldn't work." By eliminating what didn't work, he discovered what would work and achieved success.

During the mid-sixties, a student at Yale University developed an innovative idea for shipping letters and packages. In a junior-year management class project, he proposed a transportation network where trucks would pick up packages and take them to a local airport to be flown to a central airport within the country. During the night, the packages would be sorted and flown again to their local destinations. The idea was overnight delivery.

Fred Smith proposed his idea in class, but his professor told him it wasn't possible. The teacher gave him a C for the project. But Mr. Smith was determined to start Federal Express. However, after graduating and trying to get the business off the ground, he plunged $30 million into debt, was indicted on bank fraud, and was sued by his family. None of those things deterred him, and with an attitude of perseverance, with a thermostat set for success, he eventually turned FedEx into a shipping behemoth.

SUCCESSFUL PEOPLE DON'T HAVE PROBLEMS THEY HAVE PROJECTS

It's been said that a setback is nothing more than a setup for a comeback. With the right attitude, the setbacks you face teach you new things and make you stronger. You come back bigger and better than you were.

When I coach people, I encourage them to stop using the word *problem*. Successful people don't have problems; they have projects. When you say, "I've got a problem," that might mean you view it as something insurmountable. Problems can be finite, final. But when you say, "I've got a project," it means you're working on it. It's something that makes you roll up your sleeves and tackle it.

When you live with a bad attitude, you become a

volunteer victim. You say, "I have to settle." But as it turns out, there is no settling in life—you're either growing or you're dying. There is no gray area. You can't hold tight to the status quo. There's only forward or backward.

When you don't move forward, all areas of your life suffer. If you're mired in the status quo at work, you can't put a firewall around your home life and separate it. If you under-perform on the job, if your boss rides your case, eventually you'll take frustrations home with you. You won't feel good about yourself. You'll go home, and you'll shout at your wife, you'll kick the dog, you'll kick your kids off your chair, and you'll get lost in front of the TV. You'll get lost watching sports or some show that makes you feel marginally alive. The only place you'll feel like a king is in that chair.

Whistle While You Work

One day, soon after my experience with Cassandra at the airport, I walked down a hall in an office building and passed a janitor, a young man, mopping the floor. He whistled and moved around quickly, standing erect with his shoulders back. He looked like a man who was happy and full of energy. He immediately attracted my attention, and I had to say something to him.

His name tag read Leonard, and after saying hello, I asked, "What's got you so happy today, Leonard?"

"Ah, I have so much to be thankful for, and this floor looks great after I clean it!" he said.

I walked out of that building with a smile on my face. His whistling, his attitude, lifted my spirits.

In fifteen years, if I track down Leonard, where do you think he'll be? There's a chance, I suppose, he'll still be washing those floors, maybe whistling, or maybe no longer whistling. But if I put money on it, I believe he'll work in one of those offices. He's going to manage something. He's going to lead people. He's going to encourage them. He will have attracted people's attention *because of his attitude.*

On the other hand, where do you think Cassandra will be? I think she'll be lucky to still have her job. Most likely, her employer will have let her go because she under-performed and people *noticed her attitude.*

NOT ONLY DOES A SUCCESS ATTITUDE LIFT US UP TO GREATER HEIGHTS, BUT IT ALSO SPREADS TO OTHER PEOPLE

Attitude will promote Leonard and demote Cassandra. My hunch is that Leonard believes he'll be successful in life. He has a passion for life. My hunch further tells me that Leonard believes he'll achieve success because he already believes he's been blessed with so much. He possesses an attitude of gratitude.

Paul said to "count it all joy." Most people passing by Leonard, I believe, would be surprised to see a janitor so content. But a fire burned in him that mere circumstances couldn't extinguish.

Just to be clear, I draw a strong distinction between contentment and complacency. Complacency is a lack of fire. It's going nowhere. Someone who is content, however, knows their current situation is temporary. "Where I am is okay," they say. "But when an opportunity comes along, I'm going after it." They don't complain. They don't play the blame game. They simply appreciate what they have. They don't live for the moment, but they maximize the moment and set their sight on the future.

If we succumb to complacency, if we dwell on our challenges and our weaknesses, in effect, we offend God. Is that what we really want to do? In *My Utmost for His Highest*, Oswald Chambers said: "The way we continually talk about our own inabilities is an insult to our Creator. To complain over our incompetence is to accuse God falsely of having overlooked us. Get into the habit of examining from God's perspective those things that sound so humble to men. You will be amazed at how unbelievably inappropriate and disrespectful they are to Him."

God wants us to have a positive attitude, not only because He's given us so much, but because our attitude affects other people.

Attitude feeds attitude. Pessimism and harmful thoughts feed off each other. Negative people attract other negative people. They gather around the watercooler and complain and gossip. Then they go home and watch the local news and unconstructive entertainment, becoming consumers of negative information so they can feel better about themselves. They feel better, not by following their passion to freedom, but by looking down on people in greater levels of slavery. They return to work and spread the negativity—unaware they're falling further into slavery themselves.

But positive energy feeds on positive energy. Our job is to be the light. Not only does a success attitude lift us up to greater heights, but it also spreads to other people. By using a success attitude to overcome obstacles, we can enter a dark place and bring hope.

I accept it as a personal challenge to keep things positive around me. When I go into a room where people complain about this or that, I offer a silver lining for them to consider. Society, in general, wants us to focus on what we don't have. It wants us to focus on what goes wrong. It's a battle, and to win, we must take a conscious approach toward attitude and not get sucked into the whining that society embraces.

Whether we like it or not, the attitudes we take influence lives every day. I, for one, want my life to shine. I want to let my life shine so other people will know their life can shine, also.

If I shine my light, maybe next time there's a disaster, I'll be able to persuade more people to move forward instead of backward. I'll be able to persuade more people to embrace the inheritance of freedom the Lord has ordained for all of us.

Ownership

PART FIVE

CHAPTER 13

To Be or Not to Be?

Sometime during the late nineteenth century, a wealthy businessman prepared for a trip out West. He planned to be gone for one year as he set up a new business in the wild and opportunistic land of California.

The man was smart and managed his many businesses wisely. He grew his income, and he controlled his expenses, hence his wealth skyrocketed. He managed his employees harshly and made sure they didn't mess up what he'd built.

As the man prepared to leave his home and board the train for the West Coast, he gathered his three personal managers together. These were men who administrated all his personal finances and properties. He gave $50,000 to one of the managers and instructed him to invest it wisely until he returned. To another manager, he gave $20,000 with the same instructions. And to the third, he gave $10,000.

The managers each took the money but they responded differently to their boss's orders. The first two managers took active responsibility for the funds. Their boss had entrusted them with something very valuable, so they took time to research the investments with the highest return, and finding them, they deposited the funds in the best opportunities. Over the course of a year, their funds doubled in value.

WE ARE MANAGERS OF HIS INHERITANCE

But the third manager didn't want responsibility for the money. He was scared. He didn't believe he was worthy of such stewardship. His circumstances and the choices he had to make overwhelmed him. Not willing to honor his boss's trust, the manager let fear overtake him. He made a choice to do nothing. He took the money and buried it in the ground behind his boss's mansion.

Of course, if you're familiar with the original version of the parable of the talents found in Matthew 25, then you know how the story turned out. The wealthy man returned after his long journey and discovered that the first two managers had doubled their investments, but the third had earned nothing. The wealthy man rewarded the first two and fired the third.

What was the difference between the managers who doubled their money and the one who didn't? None of them knew the wealthy man was going to dump that responsibility on them. All of them knew the wealthy man was a harsh task manager, but the first two made a choice to not let their circumstances control them. They took ownership of their job. The third manager abandoned ownership of his responsibilities, and ultimately, he abandoned ownership of his life. In my story, the manager lost his job, his livelihood. In the Bible, the wealthy man ordered that the third "worthless" servant be thrown "outside, into the darkness, where there will be weeping and gnashing of teeth."[1]

God has given each of us something very valuable. We are managers of His inheritance, and we are trusted to not only honor that inheritance, but we are instructed to expand it. We are instructed to take ownership of it, not to run from it. We are tasked with making choices, confronting challenges, making necessary changes, and ultimately growing what He has given us.

In the parable, the wealthy man takes the money from the third servant and gives it to the first. The same thing happens in life: the people who take the most ownership of their lives experience the most success, whereas the people who run from life end up losing everything—even what, through fear, they tried so hard to hold on to.

Directing Your Play

Life is a skill, but it's a learned skill. In every aspect of your life, you learned how to live by working through circumstances and by watching other people. You didn't receive a manual with step-by-step instructions on how to be a parent, or how to get a college degree, or how to master a certain job. It all had to be learned.

When we face new circumstances, we must make one of two choices: either we apply ourselves to mastering those circumstances, or we surrender ourselves to those circumstances in hopes they'll go away on their own. Unfortunately, circumstances never go away by ignoring them. Instead, we are forced to confront them over and over, becoming enslaved to them until we summon the willpower to break free. Getting stuck is a sure sign we're not making the proper choices.

We must take ownership of our lives by treating freedom as an ongoing project. We must remember Socrates words about how we shouldn't live an unexamined life. At the end of every day, we need to have a conversation with ourselves and ask: *What things worked? What things didn't work?* We have to take an honest inventory of how we confront our circumstances and, where necessary, make different choices and appropriate changes.

YOU ARE THE PLAYWRIGHT, YOU ARE THE DIRECTOR, AND YOU ARE THE STAR

You must take ownership of your dream. You must take ownership of that incredibly valuable vision God implanted in you. You must do all you can, with all you have, from where you are.

God created us as masters—to have dominion over the earth. He did not create us as leaves blowing in the wind. We are conquerors. When I give a speech, sometimes I'll ask the audience to lift up their hands, look at them, and recall that old children's song *He's Got the Whole World in His Hands*. That song spoke to God's sovereignty, but in a much smaller but still significant way, we hold our world in our hands. I tell them, "Your success or failure is in your hands. It's at your fingertips."

Work, money, or a relationship can enslave us because we fail to grasp the power of choice. Another philosopher, Plato, said: "Life must be lived as a play." You live in your own play: you are the playwright, you are the director, and you are the star. But too many of us give the author's pen and the director's chair to someone else. We allow "society" or "the odds" to determine our destiny, and like a slave master, to take ownership of our lives.

Each day we live will never come around again. Each trip around the sun is either an opportunity gained or an opportunity lost. Freedom becomes possible when we realize that fact, and dedicate ourselves to grabbing the once-in-a-lifetime opportunities that happen every day.

In *Your Road Map for Success*, John Maxwell said: "The only true freedom each of us has in life is the freedom to choose. The most important choice is who we will become." The secret to success comes down to challenges, choices, and changes.

Challenges will come. They always do. But you must take ownership of your dream, and make the proper choices and changes that will convert your dream to reality.

When we think of Michael Jordan, it's hard to imagine that he was once cut from his high school varsity basketball team. He wasn't good enough; he didn't make the grade. But after getting cut, he made a choice to continue practicing and to practice harder than he ever had. He made a decision to improve as a player and change the weaknesses that led to his failure. He practiced every day. He practiced early in the morning and late at night. The coach often had to kick him out of the gym and send him on to class.

Like Jordan, you have to work your game. You have to work your craft, your trade. If you're a singer, and you don't make the first musical, you can get yourself a voice coach. If you're a businessman, and you don't land the plum job, you can research what it takes to get that job and go out and make it happen. You don't ever have to voluntarily relinquish something you own.

It's like renting an apartment versus owning a home.

When we buy a home, we do the research. We determine the good neighborhoods to live in, the good schools, etc. Then, once we take possession of our sought-after home, we value it. We take care of it. We do the regular maintenance. We plant shrubs. We build up equity in the house. We treat it as a long-term project.

But when we rent an apartment, we make a minimal effort to find something that meets our short-term needs. We don't care about the long term; we'll move again before long and reinvent our life once more. We also don't take care of an apartment like a home. We leave the maintenance to someone else. We put nicks in the walls and assume the deposit will cover it when we move out. Simply put, we don't value the place.

Remember how we joke when we're driving a rental car, and we hit a large pothole that shakes the entire frame? When we hit a pothole with our own car, we anxiously listen to make sure our car is okay. But when it's a car from Avis, we smile at our passenger and say, "Ah, it's just a rental!"

Are you owning your life or are you simply renting the life that you stumbled into?

The Real Thing

Russell Simmons, the owner of Phat Farm, wrote a book with a great title: *Do You!: 12 Laws to Access the Power in You to Achieve Happiness and Success.* Do you! That's a great title because that's our call in life.

Shakespeare's Hamlet asked the question: "To be, or not to be?" Are you going to be you, or are you not? Are you going to own up to your dream, and do what must be done to make that dream a reality?

You must determine who you are, what you are, and where you are, and operate from that perspective. Too many people come up to me after I speak and say, "Ken, I want to be just like you someday." I know they're trying to be nice and complimentary, but that's such a bad mindset to have. It devalues who they are. It devalues who God created them to be.

No matter where we are in life, no matter what level we're on, we made an appointment to be there. By the thoughts we chose and the actions we took, we determined our location. We are the sum of our choices.

When we try to be like somebody else, we're just an imitation. If you buy an imitation Gucci purse or a knockoff Rolex watch, the product is cheaper. It's not made to the same standards. It's not the real thing.

WE ARE THE SUM OF OUR CHOICES

When I was a boy, I wanted desperately to become a professional basketball player. As the old slogan said, I wanted to "be like Mike." I tried out for the basketball team, and I worked my heart out during camp. The coach even singled me out as someone who had the drive every player needed to make the team and win games. I was stoked. I knew I was going to make the team. I had what it took.

But I didn't make the team. I was shocked when I read the roster and didn't see my name.

Like Michael Jordan, however, I redoubled my efforts. I practiced and practiced, and the following year, I went out for the team—again. This time I was a better player and was more prepared. But unlike Mike, I didn't make the team that year, either. Nor did I make it the year after that.

To be honest, I wasn't built like a basketball player.

I was short and a bit pudgy. I admitted that I didn't possess the gifts necessary to overcome those weaknesses. I couldn't be like Mike.

Soon, however, I learned that I possessed different gifts. I had gifts suited to the food industry, as well as to encouragement and motivation. When I discovered those gifts, they grew even bigger, and I worked to become the masterpiece God had ordained.

WE ARE NOT SHACKLED TO A LIFE THAT IS GETTING US NOWHERE

No one can run my race for me. People can coach me, guide me, edify me, but at the end of the day, I have to go through the exercises and the struggle. I can't cross the finish line unless I make the choices necessary to get there.

Many people don't recognize their own value. How many times do people apply for a job, and when they fill out the application, they write "Negotiable" under "DESIRED SALARY"? They don't know what they're worth, and they sell themselves short.

When we change the way we look at something, the thing we look at begins to change. When we make monsters out of our obstacles, or we pursue a path that God didn't intend for us, we get stuck. But when we change our response, we see the truth better. We see that the obstacles can be overcome or we see that the direction we're following is a false path.

I believe life is like poker. When it deals us a bad hand, we can throw our cards in and eventually get another hand. We're not shackled to a life that's getting us nowhere.

The Lord has placed a path before us, and He wants us to stay in our lane. If we change lanes, we'll get stuck in the mud or face a head-on collision. Then, we'll experience disappointment, pain, and suffering. But if we take possession of our lane and commit to it, if we value who we are, then we'll know the freedom of the open road, and we'll reach our destination.

Our Lord is a God with unlimited wealth, and He's given us something valuable to invest. It's our job to take ownership of that investment and make it grow.

(Footnotes)
[1] Matthew 25:30

CHAPTER 14

Sweat the Small Stuff

Bishop Paul Morton leads the Greater St. Stephen Full Gospel Baptist Church in New Orleans. Since he was called there in 1972, the church has grown from 700 members to 20,000 members. To the eyes of everyone who followed him, Bishop Morton is an amazing success.

But like all of us, his life has had its rough moments. During his career, he experienced a mental breakdown, the loss of his infant grandchild, and colon cancer. But with God's help, he recovered from those traumas. Then came Katrina, the disaster that shook his life to the core.

He lost his home and his cars. The lives of friends and family members were destroyed. His church building was ruined and members scattered across the country. Everything he had built came crashing down.

It would've been easy for Bishop Morton to run away and hide after the tragedy, but instead, he took ownership of his situation. He worked to reconnect his members who were now dispersed across thirty-two states. He offered words of support. He encouraged his members to praise and pray their way through the struggle. He acted as a community leader, helping to rebuild the city, and declared that New Orleans would not be defeated.

After the personal struggles Paul Morton had experienced, it would've been easy to check out of life after Katrina. It would've been easy for those life-changing events to become his master, but Jesus Christ is the master of Bishop Morton, and Morton couldn't turn away from his master.

Bishop Morton is also an inspiring singer, and he recently released a new CD titled, *I'm Still Standing*. Out of his Katrina experience, his CD offers his heartfelt testimony of hope and love. As a leader in a crisis, he understood that he had to take ownership and *be* the change he wanted to see take place.

As a preacher, Bishop Morton understood that ownership started with the smallest of things; namely, thoughts and words.

When we consider taking ownership of our lives, we tend to think about the big things—taking responsibility for our vision and our purpose. And we must certainly do that, but ownership begins in the smallest of moments; it begins by owning every minute of every day.

Eternity is in every minute, because that's where we develop the thoughts and words that, over time, make up our success. Of course, we don't always have control over how we spend every minute. But we do possess total control over the thoughts and words we put into each of those minutes.

Our minds are like a refrigerator. My wife buys our

food at Costco every month, but she has to watch the size of the things she buys because they have to fit in our refrigerator. Just like our minds, it has a limited capacity.

Our thoughts sometimes have a mind of their own; they can wander in unpredictable directions. However, we can control the thoughts we keep and focus on; the thoughts we store inside us.

Our thoughts lead to our actions. If we fill our brains with negative ideas and negative images, eventually we'll fill to capacity, and there won't be room for anything positive. Negative thoughts will lead to negative actions. By taking ownership of our thoughts, we proactively discard the ones that will only fight against our life of freedom.

WHEN YOU GET RID OF STINKING THINKING, YOUR FAITH ELEVATES TO THE NEXT LEVEL

Your faith will work hand in hand with your thoughts. When you get rid of stinking thinking, your faith elevates to the next level. New possibilities, once thought impossible, now become probable.

Thoughts and Words

People look to other people to lift them up, and there are many encouragers in the world who play a major role in helping to lift people out of their troubles. But that can't ever happen without us owning our lives from the bottom up. Positive change doesn't take place from the top down; nobody can force us to be successful.

When I was a child—living in poverty and facing eviction after eviction—my mother insisted that we never have a poverty mentality. She offered words of encouragement, telling us, "God promised you as far as your eyes can see." Unfortunately, there were plenty of other people around us who insisted that things would never get better—that people in poverty were meant to stay in poverty.

Faced with conflicting thoughts from different directions, I had a choice of which thoughts to keep in my head—the positive ones or the negative ones. That was my first step in taking ownership of my life.

If you want to change your circumstances in addition to your thoughts, you also have to change the way you talk. Words are the most powerful things on this planet.

In Genesis, what did God use to create day and night?

That's right: words. "God said, 'Let there be light'; and there was light."[1] And it didn't stop with light. Land, oceans, trees, creatures, men—God used words to bring all His creations into being. He spoke them into existence.

Even Jesus Christ is intertwined with the sacredness of words. In John, it says: "In the beginning was the Word, and the Word was with God, and the Word was God. He was in the beginning with God."[2] So there's no mistaking the significance of the Word, John tells us: "And the Word became flesh and dwelt among us, and we beheld His glory, the glory as of the only begotten of the Father, full of grace and truth."[3]

However, the power of words was not left just to God and His Son. Although we won't design a universe through speaking words of creation, we can create our own universe through ownership of the words we speak.

In Charles Capps's book *God's Creative Power Will Work for You*, a little book, which has sold millions of copies, Capps says: "Your words have power. Your words are the most powerful thing in the universe today. They are containers of power. Many people have been defeated in life because they believe and have spoken the wrong things. They allowed the words of their mouth to hold them in bondage."

Bondage or freedom? The choice you make in answer to that question begins with the choice you make in the words you use. They are the seeds you plant.

Jesus taught us, "If you say to this mountain, 'Be removed and be cast into the sea,' it will be done."[4] Not only did He think words were powerful enough to move mountains, but He clearly stated that the power of words was available for all to use.

I believe in the power of words, and I hear people speaking their destinies into reality every day. Unfortunately, the destinies they often create are not the destinies that God has in mind.

I hear: "I'll never find a husband." "All women are worthless." "I'm stuck in this job forever." "The economy is bad. My business is going to fail." They're like those Israelites, spying out Canaan, who saw themselves as grasshoppers. The Israelites spoke words of personal insignificance, and they all ended up dying. People, today, speak words of personal insignificance, and their freedom dies.

Many of us speak evil to our children. In moments of anger and frustration, we tell them, "You're not going to amount to anything." "You're just like your father." "You're dumb as a rock." When we speak harsh words like those to children, we become the prophet over their lives.

Remember that old saying from childhood: "sticks and stones may break my bones, but words will never hurt me"? That's a lie from the pit of hell. Negative words hurt. They destroy.

When an adult tells a child he or she won't amount

to anything, the power of words has an uncanny way of making that prediction come true. But tell a child that he or she will do great things—that God has a wonderful future in store; that she has amazing talents that will do great good—and the power of words will make those predictions come true, also.

Peter tells us: "He who would love life and see good days, let him refrain his tongue from evil, and his lips from speaking deceit."[5] Negative words are the enemy of life and good days. As with children, you are also the prophet of your own life. You must speak the words of your vision. If you hesitate, if you are afraid to speak words of confidence and affirmation because you worry they won't come true, then you're not taking ownership of your vision. You're simply renting it; trying it on for size.

YOU MUST SPEAK THE WORDS OF YOUR VISION

When I was working my way up through the food industry, I spoke the words, "I'm going to own a restaurant." I spoke them often and out loud. I had to believe them, *and* I had to speak them. When you put your dreams into the universe, and your actions line up with your dreams, they manifest themselves. To be effective in life, you must speak, audibly speak, words of faith. Paul said: "Let no corrupt word proceed out of your mouth, but what is good for necessary edification, that it may impart grace to the hearers."[6]

Ruler Over Many Things

Once we take ownership of our thoughts and words, we can then take ownership of our habits—the physical building blocks of our success. For people who are stuck, often it's their habits, the little, seemingly innocent things they do each day that prevent them from moving forward. The oversleeping, the overspending, the television watching—these and so many other bad habits drag us down.

In the early days of hot air balloon travel, balloon pilots had to use sandbags to control their takeoff. They'd tie sandbags to the sides of the basket, and when the balloon needed to go higher, the pilot would start dropping the sandbags to the ground. In a similar way, we are like hot air balloons; when you want to soar, you have to take ownership of your habits and discard the ones that weigh you down.

TO BE SUCCESSFUL, WE HAVE TO TAKE 100% RESPONSIBILITY FOR EVERYTHING IN OUR LIVES

Make a list of the habits that stand in the path of your dreams. Ownership requires honesty, so you have to be blunt with yourself. Some of those habits might be hard to give up. You might have to surrender music you enjoy, but infiltrates your thoughts with negative messages. You might have to give up hanging with friends that don't think your dreams stand a chance.

Then, with our thoughts, words, and habits reformed around freedom instead of slavery, our faith explodes and our confidence grows. That confidence then encourages us to take even more ownership over our lives.

To be successful, we have to take 100 percent responsibility for everything in our lives—our successes and our failures. Everything.

Too many people play the blame game. They have to

find somebody whose actions are responsible for the road-blocks they face. If they can't avoid destructive behaviors, they blame their parents and their upbringing. If they don't get the promotion, they blame their boss. If their marriage falls apart, they blame their spouse. And if recent lawsuits are any indication, if they gain weight, they blame fast food restaurants.

I once coached a man who was struggling with debt. He claimed that he couldn't improve his situation because the credit card companies kept sending him applications. "How can I get out of debt if the credit companies won't leave me alone?" He allowed himself to apply for credit, but he still blamed the companies.

"You can't complain about something you allow," I told him.

We get passed over for a promotion because we don't excel at everything we do, and we allow other people to outperform us. We lose our marriage because, regardless of our spouse's behavior, we allow pride and anger to take over our heart. We gain weight because we allow ourselves to come home and drop onto the recliner and pick up the remote.

When we take ownership of our success, we can't blame other people for our problems because we don't allow other people control over our lives. We don't open the door and let them in. If we fail at something, we say, "That didn't work out. What are the lessons for me? What can I change next time? What are my opportunities?"

We don't look at people who succeed and say, "He got favor," as if he received some random blessing. Remember what the wealthy man said in the parable of the talents to the servants who doubled their talents? "Well done, good and faithful servant," he said. "You were faithful over a few things, I will make you ruler over many things. Enter into the joy of your Lord."[6] Ownership starts with being faithful over a few things and expanding that to every part of our lives. As we grow in faith, the Lord increases our dominion and our joy.

It is time to enter into the joy of our Lord. It is time to take ownership of our lives. The moving van has pulled into the driveway. The door is open. It's time to take possession and take complete responsibility. Our thoughts, our words, our habits—these are all tools that will propel us along the journey of success.

(Footnotes)
[1] Genesis 1:3
[2] John 1:1-2
[3] John 1:14
[4] Matthew 21:21
[5] Ephesians 4:29
[6] Matthew 25:21,23

CHAPTER 15

Holy, Acceptable

The Lord gives us a life, and we give it back to the Lord by serving Him. But we can't give what we don't possess. We must own our life. Only by owning our life, can we, as Paul says: "present your bodies a living sacrifice, holy, acceptable to God, which is your reasonable service."[1] We are to present our entire beings—our whole life as it is—to God, and through that sacrifice, let Him be our master.

Paul adds: "Do not be conformed to this world, but be transformed by the renewing of your mind, that you may prove what is that good and acceptable and perfect will of God."[2] Complete ownership requires transformation. As I wrote in the previous chapter, ownership begins with your thoughts and words, which then leads to taking responsibility for every practical aspect of your life—your job, relationships, finances, and health.

Jesus reminds us that "no one puts new wine into old wineskins; or else the new wine bursts the wineskins, the wine is spilled, and the wineskins are ruined. But new wine must be put into new wineskins."[3] When we're ready and committed to a new life of freedom, we can't put that new life (the new wine) into an old lifestyle (an old wineskin). Otherwise, the new life will be lost.

Ownership of Our Job

We must address each facet of our life and determine how we plan to take 100 percent responsibility for it. In our careers, for example, we'll find different ways to take ownership depending on the unique characteristics of our job. But there are some general ways we all can take responsibility at work.

WE NEED TO OWN THE IMPRESSION WE GIVE OTHERS

First, we must manage how we appear to our colleagues; we must do the small things right. We need to arrive at work on time every day. We need to dress well. We need to be polite and enthusiastic. We need to avoid the "blame gamers" who gather around the watercooler each day to whine and complain. In the bigger scheme of things, we must do the work that's expected of us—plus more. In fact, when I coach people on their careers, I encourage them to make themselves overqualified for their job. "Do your boss's job," I say. "You can't want your boss's job someday if you don't already know how to do it."

When I worked at Lorenzo's Restaurant in Chicago, I viewed myself as the owner of a business. The actual owner, Ted Rafokolis, paid the bills and put a roof over my business, but as far as my tables went, it was my restaurant to run. I learned how the kitchen operation ran; I learned how the front house operation ran. I worked hand in hand with every person in the place. I took responsibility for every aspect of the service my customers received. There was no function in the restaurant that I didn't understand and contribute to in some way.

Ownership of Our Relationships

Taking ownership of our careers is just one element of achieving success, however. Success requires balance and balance requires that we treat all aspects of our life with the same reverence and responsibility.

We've seen plenty of statistics about our country's high divorce rate. Even worse, according to some surveys, the numbers are even higher for Christians. We go out into the world to serve God, and many of us don't even take care of our own household.

Mother Teresa said: "It is easy to love the people far away. It is not always easy to love those close to us . . . Bring love into your home for this is where our love for each other must start." To serve God and learn how to love one another, we must bring love into our homes. We must take ownership of our family relationships.

Taking ownership of our relationships doesn't mean, however, that we focus on what we get out of them. On the contrary, good relationships require that we first seek to understand before seeking to be understood. In my marriage, my job is to edify my wife. She edifies me as well, and it results in a domino effect. We both take care of each other's needs, and we don't have to worry about our own needs being met.

Whenever Deidre and I had a disagreement early in our marriage, I'd tell her, "You don't understand me." I'd focus exclusively on myself. But as I later worked to understand her better, something unexpected happened. She became less vulnerable, and she understood me better.

Successful individuals not only enjoy a strong relationship with their spouse, but they also take ownership for having a healthy bond with their children. When we want to own something in the material world, we need to give our money. But when we take ownership over our relationships, we need to give our time. As Deidre so bluntly reminded me, your family requires your presence, not your presents.

WHEN WE TAKE OWNERSHIP OVER OUR RELATIONSHIPS, WE NEED TO GIVE OUR TIME

We cannot buy a true family, as much as we cannot buy true friendship.

When we consider the number of troubled kids today, we tend to blame the media, television, and video games. Those are certainly problems, but parents can generally keep their kids away from those influences. My boys play video games, but they play Pac Man and Mario Brothers. We won't let them play anything else. Hip-hop is responsible for using the N-word and the B-word, but parents are responsible for what their kids download on their iPods. Parents determine what their kids watch on television.

Neglect and indifference contribute much more to kids going bad than any of the entertainment world's influences. The most precious thing we have to offer is time. The clock always ticks. We can never replace the minutes that have passed us by.

If you seek to take 100 percent responsibility for your relationships, then you must make your investments in time—both now and in the future. As we journey along the road of success, as I discovered, the temptation to exchange presence for presents becomes even greater. To accomplish greater achievements, we feel we must sacrifice our time with family and friends for greater focus on work. But that leads to an imbalanced life, and most assuredly, failure in God's eyes.

CONTROLLED SPENDING IS THE SECRET TO ACHIEVING WEALTH

When relating to a family member, a friend, a business partner, an employee, whomever—we must remember Christ's words about who would be the greatest: "If anyone desires to be first, he shall be last of all and servant of all."[4] Ownership of relationships requires servanthood. We want to be exalted, but Scripture tells us that the proud will be humbled and the humble will be exalted.

We have to be careful. As we climb the ladder of success, we must remember that Jesus came down to us. He came from heaven to earth to serve and wash the feet of those who will follow. While we're so focused on going up, we might miss Him as He comes down. We might find ourselves going in the opposite direction of Christ.

Ownership of Our Finances

We can also take ownership of our lives by serving God as our master and not allowing something else to control us. Specifically, poor money management causes many people to voluntarily enslave themselves to a false master.

To take ownership over your finances, you must know your income and take a close look at your expenses. When people struggle with money, they often look at their income and determine how they can generate more. They take on a second job, or their spouse goes to work. But the problem doesn't improve because they don't learn to control their spending. Their income goes up and their expenses rise to match it.

Controlled spending is the secret to achieving wealth. Our expenses must fall under our income. To do that, at least in the beginning when we're developing new habits, we need to cut up the credit cards. Anybody who's trying to rise to the next level in financial freedom must get rid of them.

If you still want purchasing flexibility without carrying around a lot of cash, then you can get a debit card. A debit card provides accountability, since it won't let you spend more than what's in your bank account. A credit card, on the other hand, will let you spend and spend and spend, and then it'll let you spend the next thirty years making minimum payments to pay it off. It will keep you in bondage; MasterCard will become your master.

When you build up a credit card balance, you make a choice to borrow from your future. Piece by piece, you chip away at the upcoming freedom that was waiting for you.

When Deidre and I started planning to buy a home, she put us on a strict cash system. In fact, she put me on envelopes! I couldn't believe it at first. She had an envelope for everything. She set aside cash for each bill and put them in envelopes. She set aside a weekly allowance for each of us to pay for gas and other expenses. It was tough, but we wanted to go from renters to owners. We had a vision. We had specific goals. And we had to take ownership of our actions.

You cannot spend more than you make and pursue God's destiny for your life. You must decide today whom you shall serve: God or goods, the Master or MasterCard. As for me and my house, we will spend less than we make, and we will serve the Lord.

There are easy things you can do to control your spending. Instead of going to Starbucks and buying that latte, you can make your coffee at home. Instead of driving to work every day, you can call someone and arrange a carpool. Instead of buying the latest fashions—marked up 100 percent because they carry a designer name—you can purchase almost-new clothes at an upscale secondhand store. Once you take ownership over finances and apply creativity to your needs, the options for spending less are limitless.

It comes back to choices. I knew if I wanted to buy a house, I couldn't go to the barbershop every week. Deidre had to paint her own nails. We couldn't go out to eat too often. By saving money and investing it in a house, we made money our slave, instead of being a slave to money. We put our money to work for us, and it now makes us even more money.

In *The Millionaire Next Door*, Thomas Stanley and William Danko conducted an extensive study of millionaires in this country. They discovered some surprising results. Many of the people we believe to be millionaires are actually people they call "big hat, no cattle." They earn a lot of money, but they spend as much as they make and end up with little appreciable wealth. They think wealth is about accumulating all the bling-bling that makes them *look* wealthy instead of actually being wealthy.

Most millionaires, Stanley and Danko found, were people who held everyday jobs or ran unglamorous businesses; they were welding contractors, rice farmers, pest controllers, paving contractors. One of the most significant common characteristics they found among those millionaires "next door" was their spending habits. They spent much less than they made, and they put their money to work in accumulating wealth.

YOUR HEALTH IS ALSO YOUR WEALTH

They understood investment principles such as the Rule of 72, for example, which states if you invest your money at a modest return, you'll double your funds in seven years. So, if you invest $500, in seven years you'll end up with $1,000. Conversely, if you spend $500 and put it on a credit card, with the usual high interest rates, you'll end up paying well over $1,000 in the same time period. With your original $500, you'll end up more than $2,000 poorer than if you'd invested it.

Ownership of Our Health

While we take ownership of our relationships and our finances, we also need to take control of our personal health. Your health is also your wealth.

In 1 Corinthians, Paul asks: "Do you not know that your body is the temple of the Holy Spirit who is in you, whom you have from God, and you are not your own?"[5] Serving God is not only a spiritual pursuit. "For you were bought at a price; therefore glorify God in your body and in your spirit, which are God's."[6]

Our spiritual lives and our bodies are entwined; hence our bodies are temples that we must treat as holy vessels. We must treat them with the utmost respect. That's why John, when writing a letter to his friend, Gaius, greeted him: "Beloved, I pray that you may prosper in all things and be in health, just as your soul prospers."[7]

Living in freedom requires that we plan for our physical well-being. If your exercise plan consists of lifting and pointing the remote, and your diet plan consists of ketchup as a primary vegetable, then you're not treating your body as a temple. Instead, you're directly contributing to health problems that will limit your freedom.

When I get up in the morning, I tithe my firstfruits of the day to God, spending time in prayer and studying the Word. But after that, I give the next time block to myself. I spend that time in exercise, so I'll be equipped to live out my purpose and serve the Lord.

But that's not the only time I exercise; I find opportunities all day to walk. You can walk up the stairs at the office instead of taking the elevator. You can park in the back of the parking lot at the supermarket instead of cruising the rows for a closer space. When you travel, you can walk between the terminals instead of taking the moving sidewalks. When it comes to exercise, there are plenty of moments to maximize the opportunity.

Likewise, when it comes to eating, most of us aren't treating our bodies as temples. We don't sit down to a table with our family to consume our meals; instead, we eat on the fly. In the fast food industry, 71 percent of customers come through the drive-thru. When we don't plan our meals, we put a priority on eating foods that are convenient instead of healthy. We can't get our allowance of vegetables if we eat five meals a week inside our car.

As with our relationships and finances, health requires balance. It's okay to eat the fun foods, but when they become our main staple, we're in trouble. Our health is going to start owning us instead of the other way around.

You must make daily deposits in your health "account." Without making daily deposits, you won't be able to make any withdrawals. You'll need a healthy body to fight the obstacles that you'll confront. And you'll need good health to do the work God has ordained for you.

When we give up ownership over our lives, we give up our power. But when we accept responsibility for every facet of our intended success, we are transformed into new creatures– new, powerful creatures. The old wineskins are thrown away. In their place, we become new wineskins, ready to hold the glory of God within us.

Then, our lives will be "a living sacrifice, holy, acceptable to God."

(Footnotes)
[1]Romans 12:1
[2]Romans 12:2
[3]Mark 2:22
[4]Mark 9:35
[5]1 Corinthians 6:19
[6]1 Corinthians 6:20
[7]3 John 1:2

Associations

PART SIX

CHAPTER 16

Pulling out the Weeds

Mike grew up in a rough area—a public housing project in a crime-ridden neighborhood. Drug deals and drive-by shootings were a normal part of life in the neighborhood—a project that went by the nickname Bad Newz. When he was born, Mike's parents were unmarried teenagers and struggled to make ends meet.

But Mike had a gift and a dream. He was a great high school football player, and he knew his gift would keep him out of trouble and take him to a brighter future. Football was his ticket away from falling victim to his environment like so many other neighborhood kids.

He focused on his vision and his gifts. He took ownership of his goals and focused on his game and his strength. He studied film and practiced hard. Through perseverance, Mike's dream came true. A major football school awarded him a scholarship, and soon he led his team to the college championship game.

Later, an NFL team drafted him as the top pick. He broke records, led his team to the playoffs, and signed lucrative endorsement deals. Kids everywhere worshiped him. Michael Vick, quarterback for the Atlanta Falcons, was the epitome of success—eventually signing a contract worth $130 million and becoming, at the time, the highest paid player in the NFL's history.

WHEN YOU DRAG AN ANCHOR ALONG WITH YOU, IT WILL EVENTUALLY PULL YOU DOWN

Michael Vick made it to the Promised Land, but, as I'm sure most of you know, he brought too much of his old baggage with him. He hung out with people from his old life—people who had criminal records, people who dragged him down and encouraged him to make poor choices.

Vick took ownership of his career, but he never took ownership of his associations. Along with his buddies, he ran an illegal interstate dog-fighting ring known as Bad Newz Kennels—the ring's name referred to that troubled childhood community of Vick and his dog-fighting friends. Vick had climbed to a great level of success, but as the name symbolized, he brought the turmoil of his past with him. When you drag an anchor along with you, it will eventually pull you down.

Vick stood to gain nothing from supporting that illegal activity. And he certainly wasn't glorifying God by abusing, torturing, and killing animals. It was all for nothing.

One of the perverse ironies of Michael Vick's crime

is that he started the ring in 2001, the same year he claimed the top spot in the NFL Draft and became an instant millionaire.

In 2007, the NFL suspended the quarterback indefinitely. At the time of this writing, the Falcons are going after $20 million they paid him in signing bonuses. His lucrative endorsements have been terminated. Banks have filed multimillion-dollar lawsuits against him. Worst of all, he's now a convicted felon—a jailbird.

Unless Vick gets his act together while in jail, he's most likely headed back to a world like the one he left. Unless he surrounds himself with positive people and constructive relationships, he'll never get a second chance.

Michael Vick can't blame the media. He can't blame racial injustice. He made the choices. He chose whom to associate with. He put himself in that jail.

In 1 Corinthians, Paul said: "Bad company corrupts good character."[1] Vick had the good character to work hard and focus on his dream. But his associations trumped his character and made his hard work worthless.

The Law of Association

The Law of Association says that you become the top five people you surround yourself with. We may have many friends, and many of those people may be quite successful, but we have to take a close look at the people with whom we spend most of our time. We must remember that time has value; it is a type of currency. When we spend it, we give up a valuable resource. If you're like most people, you spend a significant majority of time with a small group of people. It's the 80/20 rule: 80 percent of our time goes to only 20 percent of our close acquaintances.

Your environment can be stronger than your will. You have to protect your vision and your gifts. They are from God, and therefore, they are holy. Since they are holy, they must be revered as the sacred objects they are. "Do not give what is holy to the dogs; nor cast your pearls before swine," Jesus said, "lest they trample them under their feet, and turn and tear you in pieces."[2]

Make no mistake. People who don't edify you, people who don't encourage your dreams will, intentionally or unintentionally, trample on your vision and tear it to pieces.

YOUR ENVIRONMENT CAN BE STRONGER THAN YOUR WILL

The people you're tight with do one of four things in your life: they add, subtract, multiply, or divide.

People who add to your life bring qualities or knowledge that you don't possess. They make you a better person—a more rounded person—and they leave you better off than when they found you. But people who subtract from your life suck the energy right out of you. They are leeches, maybe friendly, but nonetheless they are people who only want to take your time or money and never offer anything in return.

Friends and family members who multiply, however, increase the reality of your vision exponentially. They are encouragers, edifiers, mentors, or coaches. They make us believe in ourselves. They set us on fire. When around them, we are like the sower that Jesus talked about. The one that sowed his seed in good soil, and it increased a hundredfold.

But the worst people in your life are the dividers. They take your talents and your purpose and trample them. Earlier I mentioned that the first two words we hear as children are *stop* and *no*. From infancy, we finely tune our ears to those words, and they have a major impact on our motivation and our faith.

Unfortunately, many people take pleasure in uttering those words regardless of our age. They are the high school friends who tell us we're acting white by earning good grades. They are the neighbors who take offense at our wanting to go to college and leave the neighborhood. They may even be the well-meaning but harmful parents who encourage us to forget our dreams and take a high-paying job. "You want to be a doctor? You can't be that," dividers say. "Look where you come from. It's impossible." They pull us back. They conquer our spirit with despondency and hopelessness.

Growing up, I called those people *haters*. They were people who seemed to hate what I wanted to do, and sometimes, they even seemed to hate me for trying to get ahead. My father called them *crabs in a barrel*—referring to the old adage about crabs kept in a barrel, and how, when one crab tries to climb out, the others will reach up, grab the one trying to escape, and pull it back down.

Since then, I've learned that those people don't really hate us. In fact, they don't know us well enough to hate us. They actually hate that they haven't discovered who they are. They haven't learned to maximize their potential, so they look at us, and they hate that they see us on fire. They hate that we have a taste of freedom, and they don't. They're jealous. Their attitude is about them; it is not about us.

Unhealthy associations are cancerous. They infiltrate deep into the core of you and spread. They can be unstoppable if not attacked. And it doesn't take a lot of exposure to kill our dreams. Sometimes all it takes is one mistake.

Environment as a Product of You

Another young man who made a terrible choice was in my local news recently. Like Vick, he was a football player. But in addition to being a star high school athlete, he was an excellent student. He was headed to college and a bright future. Although he had never been in trouble with the law, he unfortunately didn't choose his friends well. He hung out with kids that, although they hadn't been gangbangers or lawbreakers, tended to do mischievous things.

One day, in a rash decision, some of his friends decided to carjack a woman coming home from work. The student didn't suggest the idea, but he did go along with it, not wanting to go against his friends. One of his friends had a gun, and tragically, he ended up shooting and killing the woman. In one disastrous instant, the star student's future was destroyed.

We can cruise at the top of our game, and still be one bad association, one bad decision away from incarceration or poverty. It's that simple. Time and time again, I see how environment overpowers will.

I've seen it with acquaintances who get married but refuse to give up their buddies from their single days of chasing women. Their buddies are still single, still chasing, and still engaging in wild behavior. One thing leads to another, and the married man gets sucked back into that life. He makes mistakes and loses his marriage because he lacks the guts to foster an environment supportive of his vision of a loving and healthy family life.

People say they're a product of their environment. That's an awful way to think. Instead, their environment should be a product of them. I once heard of a study that determined we need to hear *yes* seventeen times to overcome one *no*. If you're like most of us, when you think about your life, your memories of people discouraging you or judging you are probably more vivid and frequent than memories of people encouraging you. Whether we like it or not, negative associations make a significant impact on our life and freedom. Therefore, it's our responsibility to take ownership of our associations. It's our responsibility to make difficult choices and to choose associations that add to and multiply our freedom.

WE MUST FORBID OURSELVES FROM ASSOCIATING WITH THE WRONG PEOPLE

In the Word, Jesus told a parable about a farmer whose fields had been covered in weeds. The farmer eventually would have to remove them. In the parable, Jesus used the farmer to represent God, and the weeds to represent those who didn't follow Him. Likewise, we are gardeners over our own fields, our own lives. In your garden, you reap what you sow, and if you don't work your garden, you can't expect to produce a harvest.

From time to time, weeds will work their way into your garden. It's natural. But when we find them infiltrating our land, we can pick them out. We can keep our garden free of invasive and harmful plants.

If we're good parents, we keep a close eye on whom our children pick as friends. We encourage our children to hang around certain people, and in some cases, we forbid them from associating with others. However, the importance of managing associations doesn't change with age. We are always susceptible to the wrong influence. In adulthood, we must forbid ourselves from associating with the wrong people—including people who don't buy into our dreams or people who know nothing about the level to which we aspire.

Even our closest family members can drain us. I once counseled a young man who was trying to get off government assistance, and I happened to ask him whom he associated with. He listed a few people and then paused as if he'd just had a revelation.

"Mr. Brown, I've been on government assistance my whole life," he said. "And I just realized that my grandmother was on welfare, my mother was on welfare, and my brother is on welfare. Most of the people I know are on welfare. It's the only thing I know because it's the only thing I see."

If our top five people include family members who don't understand our vision and can't see the possibilities, then we have to manage their influence on our lives as well. Obviously, if we love them, we're not going to shut them out. We're not going to yank them out with the weeds. But we might need to minimize how much time we spend with them. We need to fill our time with people who are already at the next level –people who get what we're about, and can push us to where we want to go.

In so many ways, our associations shape our world. They can shine a spotlight on our vision or cover it in darkness. They can ignite our passion or douse it in a flood of cold water. They can pull us away from personal responsibility, or they can hold us accountable to ownership.

No one is too important, rich, or famous to avoid the influence of others. One of the most talented athletes in the world—a man earning $130 million, a man admired by millions of adults and children—was not strong enough to avoid people sucking him into the pit of failure. The Law of Association prevails. It's our job to take ownership over those associations and keep our garden free and healthy.

(Footnotes)
[1] 1 Corinthians 15:33 (NIV)
[2] Matthew 7:6

CHAPTER 17

Flying with the Eagles

As I moved through my career and pursued my dream of restaurant ownership, I felt drawn to people who believed in my vision and held me accountable. One such person was Archie Tolar. A friend of mine from college, Archie was also a Food and Nutrition major with an entrepreneurial spirit.

At one point, Archie and I formed a consulting business, and we were bold enough to try selling our services to McDonald's. I attended a McDonald's open house to offer our services. But unexpectedly, the company expressed an interest in hiring me, instead.

At first, I laughed at the prospect of joining McDonald's. I had already worked in fast food. I now had a great job in the supplier segment of the food industry, not to mention Archie and I had just started a consulting business on the side.

But Archie didn't laugh at the idea. "I don't know why you think it's funny," he said. "I know you. You'll go in that company and work your way up quickly. You'll own three McDonald's in three years."

I laughed. "Yeah, right. You're crazy."

"I'm okay with it. You should talk to them."

You see, Archie believed in me. He edified me, and he held me accountable.

He believed in me so much, he was willing to give up our consulting venture for me to fulfill my dream. He believed in me so much, he could see an opportunity when I couldn't. McDonald's didn't fit my preconceived path to my dream. But Archie saw how it could work, and as it turned out, he was quite prophetic in what he saw.

My ego got in the way, but Archie held me accountable. I was pregnant with my dream, but I needed help to make it happen. It's clear to me that it wouldn't have happened the way it did if not for Archie's support. He midwifed my dream.

I mentioned earlier that having a vision is like being pregnant. I understand that image requires a leap of imagination for us men, but the analogy works. We have a dream that's growing inside of us, and we need help to give it birth. We need someone holding our hand, encouraging us, telling us we can do it. We need a midwife who will guide us through the process. We need specialists, experts, who will enlighten us.

Women don't have babies by themselves. They have them with a lot of help. Even before the advent of hospitals and doctors, people gathered around a woman in labor to help her with her task.

You can't be pregnant with a vision and hang

around people who are satisfied where they are, and who are content to have you hang around with them. You need a dream team of individuals who will operate as your support group– people who are at the level you aspire to, or who are moving up to the next level alongside you. People who will stay up late talking to you on the phone when you doubt yourself and feel like quitting. People who will say, "No, you can't quit! You've got too much riding on this. Success is in you!"

You need friends and colleagues who will energize you, propel you, understand you, hold you accountable, restore your faith, and hold your hand when you leave the familiar for the unfamiliar. You need people who are fire starters instead of firefighters.

YOU NEED A DREAM TEAM OF INDIVIDUALS WHO WILL OPERATE AS YOUR SUPPORT GROUP

Forward Motion

We have a limited capacity for relationships. We're like the size of my refrigerator, which limits how many groceries Deidre can purchase. If we decide to invest time in associations compatible with our life of freedom, then we'll have to make difficult choices. To a large degree, we'll have to change our friendships. The typical person is not following his or her dreams; they're not living a life of freedom. Life is living them. If you want to succeed, then you'll have to hang around people who want to be successful, people who are going in the same direction you are. In the Bible, when Mary became pregnant, she went with haste to her cousin Elizabeth's home. Mary was pregnant, and she needed to be with someone who was in the same situation, who was headed in the same direction.

Every day, we must take a look at the direction we're headed. If we spend our days working toward our dream, but we spend our evenings with people who don't support us, then we're taking one step forward and one step back. Worse, if we spend our days only dreaming and taking no ownership over our vision, and we spend time with people who don't support us, then we're taking no steps forward and one step back. We're moving backward.

Forward is the direction we should always be moving. We're like a car driving up the ramp in a parking garage. To get to the next level we have to look forward. Ever notice how large a car's windshield is and how small the rearview mirror is? Every once in a while, we can look in the mirror at the people in the backseat and smile, or we can make a passing glance at where we've been, but the windshield draws our eyes forward. The windshield makes room for the focus of our attention.

It's critical that we make room for new people in our life who'll keep our focus forward. In 1 Corinthians, Paul said: "When I was a child, I spoke as a child, I understood as a child, I thought as a child; but when I became a man, I put away childish things."[1] We have to "put away" those things—those thoughts, habits, and people—who would keep us in the backward ways of our spiritual youth.

As I've said, people come into our lives for a reason, a season, or a lifetime. Most people come into our lives for a reason or season, but we have a tendency to make people *lifers* when God planned our time with them as temporary.

At the end of every week, I pick up my cell phone, and I scan through the list of contacts. I stop at each person and ask myself, *Are they adding, subtracting, multiplying, or dividing?* If they're not adding or multiplying, I push delete. My phone asks: "Are you sure you want to delete?" And I answer *yes*, and bam, they're gone.

It might sound cold, but we need to do that with our phone numbers *and* with the time we spend with people. Are they adding or multiplying? That doesn't mean you can't love them. It doesn't mean you can't be friendly. We are to be good Christians with all people; we are even to love our enemies. But when we're pregnant, we are vulnerable. We can't be around certain people during that time.

If a strong sense of loyalty discourages you from breaking free of certain people, what you're feeling is natural. I admire you for your loyalty, especially if you came from humble beginnings and feel an allegiance to people who "knew you when." However, the best thing you can do to help the unsuccessful, and the poor, is not to be one of them.

If you really love your family and friends, and want to help them, then you have to get free. You have to break out of your comfort zone.

After returning from a trip to Africa, Oprah Winfrey, who's done much for the world's poor, was asked if she felt guilty about her wealth. "No, I don't," she said. "I do not know how me being destitute is going to help them."

We have to understand the proper order of things. First, we learn how to live in freedom everyday, and then we bring that way of life to those we love. It's like when you're on an airplane, and the flight attendant instructs you, in case of emergency, to put the oxygen mask over your face first and *then* the face of your child. We can't bring freedom without being free ourselves.

At this point in my life, there are only a few friends from my past that I can't go around anymore. By and large, I can hang with almost all of my friends and family because I'm a different creature than I once was. My baby has been birthed into the universe. If I go to a friend who needs help, I can be a ray of hope for them.

After you've made it to the other side—when you're a new creature and strong in yourself—then you can look back. In fact, then it's vitally important that you look back and help other people along.

I was hired and mentored at McDonald's by Edie Waddell—one of the most gifted business executives I've ever known. She heard me talking about my dream, and she believed in me. She guided me through the corporation. She advised me and held me accountable to the high expectations she had for me.

WE CAN'T BRING FREEDOM WITHOUT FREEING OURSELVES

When I purchased my stores, I asked her, "How can I ever repay you for what you've done? My debt to you is so great."

"The way you repay me," she said, "is that once you succeed, you do the same thing I did for you for someone else."

After you've delivered your baby, you have to turn around and help other people who are pregnant. You have to tell them your story. If they have a dream, if you see potential in them, then you must edify them, lift them up, and do what you can to make their vision come true.

After you've delivered your baby, you can also return to some of those negative-oriented friends and family. You're no longer as vulnerable, so you can turn back to those people you truly love. However, you must always be on guard. The Lord won't let you rest for long. After a while, there will be a new level to climb to, a new baby to deliver. As I've said, success is a journey and not a destination. You'll always need to surround yourself with people who will move with you along that journey.

Success Leaves Clues

My son once owned a goldfish, and we learned that a goldfish will grow to the size of its bowl, the size of its environment. So, we took the fish out of the smaller bowl and put in into a bigger tank, and over time, it started to grow. That's what happens with us. We either shrink or grow according to our environment. With positive people joining us on the journey, we grow to match the energy they give off.

Success leaves clues. We have to watch the habits of successful people—the words they use, and how they conduct themselves.

There's an old story I've told my children about an eagle in a chicken coop. Once there was an eagle egg that fell from its nest and rolled away. When the eaglet hatched, it found its way to a chicken coop where it was surrounded by chickens. It grew up and thought it was a chicken; it walked like a chicken and clucked like a chicken. But every so often, the eaglet would see other eagles flying overhead and something stirred inside him—a desire, a passion for flying. He watched the eagles and studied how they flew. Sometimes he flapped his wings. Then one time, seeing the eagles again, he flapped his wings so hard that he left the ground. He left the chicken coop and rose to the world he was destined to inhabit.

When we decide to stop hanging around with the chickens and fly with the eagles, success will be within our reach. My friend, George Fraser, author of *Success Runs in Our Race* and founder of the PowerNetworking Conference, says: "Your network determines your net worth." Do you ever notice how wealthy or successful people seem to always hang together? They share their ideas and practices, and as a group, they acquire even more wealth and success.

Proverbs 27:17 says: "As iron sharpens iron, so a man sharpens the countenance of his friend." The wealthy congregate together, and they sharpen each other. In recent months, the sports press has reported on Tiger Woods' friendship with Roger Federer—the world's number one golfer hangs with the world's number one tennis player. They're both at the top of their game; they're peers, and they can keep each other sharp.

EVERY SINGLE PERSON WHO EXPERIENCES SUCCESS HAS DONE IT WITH THE HELP OF MANY PEOPLE

When you look at other people to include in your network, however, it's important to include more than one person. We have a tendency to apply hero-worship status to individuals and expect them to be all things. But everyone has strengths and weaknesses. People have value, but their greatest value comes in different ways.

For me to be a complete man, I know I need to have certain people in my life. One friend might be good at finances, and when I'm with him, we tend to talk about finances. He shares what practices work and helps lead me along the road of financial freedom. Another person might have been married for fifty years and have a fantastic relationship with his wife. By being around him, I pick up the thoughts and habits of someone who understands family success. Other people are role models in other ways, and from each of them, I adopt the traits I need to pursue my purpose in life.

I've experienced success with the help of many people. Every single person who's experienced success has done it with the help of many people. The world is full of Archie Tolars who can lift us up and accompany us along our journey.

It's our job to break from our comfort zones and find the associations that are waiting for us—the associations that are part of the Lord's masterpiece, part of His plan for the world and our place in it.

(Footnotes)
[1] 1 Corinthians 13:11

CHAPTER 18

The Teamwork of Dream Work

In addition to owning a restaurant, another dream of mine has been to own a hotel. I've worked in the hotel industry, and like restaurant work, serving people through hospitality had ignited my passion.

But if I were to become a hotel owner, I knew I'd have to climb to another level in my personal development. To do that, I would have to develop new associations.

Often the first place, in any given field, to literally find new associations is to contact an industry association. I researched hotel associations on the Internet and found the National Association of Black Hotel Owners, Operators, and Developers—or NABHOOD for short.

I called NABHOOD. "I'm going to be a hotel owner," I told them, "and I'd like to join your organization." Before I knew it, they inundated me with valuable information on hotel training programs, hotel ownership support resources, and conference information. It was a gold mine of material.

The annual conference looked impressive, so Deidre and I decided to attend the upcoming one in Atlanta. We didn't go there to buy a hotel; we weren't ready for that. But we wanted to interact within the atmosphere of hotel owners. We wanted to see what they talked about, how they acted, what they experienced. We felt a passion to take the next leap, and we wanted to surround ourselves with people who felt the same passion –people who were equally yoked with us.

In July 2006, we traveled to Atlanta and immersed ourselves in the conference. The energy was electric. Bob Johnson, Chairman of BET, attended the conference, along with many high-level African-American hotel executives and owners. Deidre and I felt like chickens looking at the eagles—watching them to figure out how to fly.

We talked to as many people as possible. Over lunch, we'd ask various owners, "How did you get started on your hotel?" They were more than happy to explain how they went about it.

We attended workshops for people who were pregnant with the same dream we had—workshops like *The ABCs of Getting in the Hotel Business*. There, we made other contacts with people at our level and with our aspirations.

The following year, we attended the next conference. We wanted more details on how to get from A to B: How do we identify a property? How do we transact the purchase? We made more contacts with people who were almost ready to make a purchase and with people who were one step ahead. The new hotel owners boosted our confidence. They showed us that it was possible; they helped us see what we could be.

Not only did we make contacts with people who traveled the same path as we did, but we made contacts with people who could help us purchase the hotel. They offered us the advice and support we needed, and within the next year, we made our dream come true.

But it never would've happened if we hadn't connected with the world of hotel ownership, and we hadn't developed associations that aligned with our dream.

Access and Accountability

Success is not an original act. It is a journey and a process, and people who achieve success understand the repeatable steps that are involved. We don't have to reinvent the wheel in order to be successful. In fact, people who try to go it alone, to reinvent the wheel, usually end up with a square wheel and a lifetime of not going anywhere a lifetime of being stuck.

WE DON'T HAVE TO REINVENT THE WHEEL IN ORDER TO BE SUCCESSFUL

Success isn't achieved through luck and we certainly don't get a manual on how to achieve it. So, we have to go out and learn. The more help we get, the more it puts us ahead of the curve. It gives us an edge compared to other people who opt to go it alone.

If someone wants to make a job change or become an entrepreneur, the first thing I suggest they do is get some experience in their field of interest. Get connected with people already working in that area.

"You can't be what you can't see," I tell them. If an

upcoming high school graduate wants to become a doctor, I ask, "How many doctors do you know?"

I recommend they work at a hospital. Volunteer if necessary. Become a candy striper; push some gurneys. All you need is access. Once they're in the environment, they can start making contacts with doctors. "What books should I read?" they can ask them. "What habits should I have? What were you doing at my age?" They can watch how doctors walk, how they talk. They can learn how to make their dream come true, and through their passion and ownership, they can make contact with people who can directly help them.

A woman I once coached felt a passion for tennis and wanted to do something entrepreneurial with that passion. "Why don't you get a job at a tennis club?" I asked. "It could be just for ten hours on the weekend, but you'd get immersed in the industry—learning what people need and making contact with experts in the field."

Do you want to become a consultant in a particular industry? Then get a job with a larger firm in that industry or even volunteer with a small, one-person firm. Do you want to pursue a second career as a teacher? Then become a substitute on your off day and talk to other teachers during lunch break.

When you associate with people who are one step ahead of you, not only do you gain the invaluable practical experience that education can't fully provide, but you learn the repeatable steps for success in your field. You learn what worked and what didn't. Most people enjoy being considered experts. When you approach others, you're bound to get tutelage from people who are willing to share their expertise.

Once you have access to experts, you can identify

people who stand out from the rest—people who live their life with passion and excellence. Those are people who can mentor you; people with whom you can have a one-on-one relationship. As you get to know them, sometimes you can approach them directly and ask if they would be your mentor. But other times, people can serve as your mentor without them even knowing it. You can watch them—the way they do things, the way they talk, the way they navigate around the company or industry—and you can make a conscious decision to say, "That's my mentor."

You can have mentors in different areas of life. In my previous book, I wrote about Chuck Goldberg, and how he was my mentor. I don't believe he even knew that until the book came out. But I admired him, and I watched him. I saw how his eyes glistened when he spoke about his wife. I saw the way he treated his father, the way he treated the business, the way he treated his employees. I saw how his people responded to him, and I said, "When I get my own business, I'm going to treat people the same way."

I didn't have to ask Chuck to be my mentor because I already enjoyed a close working relationship with him. But it was still important to make the conscious decision to put him in that role. That decision focused my attention on his habits and focused my attention on developing the skills he possessed.

We shouldn't shy away from asking people to be a role model for us, however. Sometimes we let our ego get in the way. We don't want to take advice, or we don't want to place ourselves in a subservient position. Other times, we let fear get in the way of approaching successful people. I've already addressed fear (false expectations appearing real) as a major stumbling block to our freedom.

If we're to obtain a life of freedom, we'll have to overcome those types of hesitations.

The idea of mentoring goes all the way back to the Bible. Paul acted as a mentor to Timothy, coaching him on how to act, what he should look out for, and encouraging him in his ministry.

When the Word says "iron sharpens iron," that represents the type of relationship Paul and Timothy had. They were both of the same mold, but Paul was further along than Timothy. Paul sharpened Timothy. He prepared him.

MENTORS, AS WELL AS PEERS OR FRIENDS, OFTEN SHARPEN US BY HOLDING US ACCOUNTABLE TO OUR DREAMS

The old saying goes: It took George Washington eight hours to cut down the cherry tree, but he spent seven of those hours sharpening his saw. Mentors are the hone or whetstone we use to sharpen our saw.

Mentors, as well as peers or friends, also sharpen us by holding us accountable to our dreams. When you associate with people who get your vision and want you to follow it, you can ask them to hold you accountable for your actions. For example, you can tell them you expect to complete a plan for a new store in six months, and you'd like them to keep tabs on you—making sure you hold to your commitments.

Deidre and I once took a wonderful vacation in Aruba. While there, we went horseback riding along the beach. It was a gorgeous setting, but I was a little intimidated by riding those large animals. *At any given moment*, I thought, *this horse can ride me out into the water*. It was a bit like starting a new business: I wanted to do it, but I also knew there were risks.

Fortunately, our guide, Miguel, told us exactly what to do. "First of all, don't let him know you're scared," he said. "Use the reins when you want him to turn. And when you want him to go, or go faster, kick him in the belly."

His last instruction made me laugh, because that's what Deidre does with me sometimes. My wife is one of my best accountability partners. When I get down, or when I'm not on top of my game, she doesn't care how I feel about it, she kicks me right in the belly. Okay, not literally, but she does look me straight in the eyes and says, "You can do better. I expect more of you, and you've got to expect more from yourself."

SUCCESS IS PERSONAL, BUT YOU CANNOT BE SUCCESSFUL BY YOURSELF

Kicking the horse in the belly doesn't hurt the horse. But it does make it go. When you surround yourself with people who care about you, *and* who care about your dreams, they can tell you the truth and it doesn't hurt. You take the licks, and you become a better person.

It Takes Help

Mentors, accountability partners, industry experts, even pastors–these are some of the associations that can form your team. Individual team members might not know they're on the team, but assimilating a dream team, at least within your mind, is critically important. Proverbs 11:14 says: "Where there is no counsel, the people fall; but in the multitude of counselors there is safety."[1]

It takes teamwork to make your dream work. Success is personal, but you cannot be successful by yourself. It is not going to happen. When someone decides to start a business, one of the first things they must do is build their infrastructure. They might need a building. They'll need suppliers. They'll need systems. Likewise, when we want to go to the next level, we have to build our personal network infrastructure.

Another person you can add to your network infrastructure is a coach. A coach is someone who's willing to make a commitment of one-on-one time to help you in your life or career. Often, we pay for a coach's services.

Michael Jordan had a coach. Hank Aaron had a coach. Wayne Gretsky. Tiger Woods. Roger Federer. The best of the best athletes all had or have coaches. They all had people who knew how to identify their strengths, and how to get the most out of them. If you observe two athletes during an off-season—one who works out on his own and the other who works with a personal trainer—the one with the trainer will make more progress.

We can engage a coach in almost any area of our life. When Deidre and I first got married and had children, we struggled to balance two careers and childrearing. So, we hired a counselor who taught us how to work together and make our partnership stronger. When I first purchased my restaurants, I hired a coach through Stephen Covey's organization who helped me balance my new entrepreneurial career and my personal life. T. D. Jakes said: "New levels bring new devils," therefore, we should engage someone at each of those levels who'll guide us beyond the reach of those devils.

Today, I work as a life coach myself, but I'm not trying to sell my services. You should find a coach who's a good match for you, and who offers the knowledge and approach that will work with your plans and personality.

To find a coach, one method I recommend is to research the coaches listed online at: christiancoachesnetwork.com or franklincoveycoaching.com.[1] You can read their bios and learn about their philosophies, values, and expertise. After researching them, I suggest you pick at least three coaches and interview them. Only by talking with them will you get a feel for who offers the best skills to assist you with your specific goals.

In addition to coaches and mentors, industry associations (such as NABHOOD) provide a network of people pursuing the same dream as you or of people who are already where you want to be. There's an association for just about any trade—there are nursing associations, carpenter associations, restaurant associations, and everything in between. Through them, you can connect with people who can bring different qualities to your dream team—financial, leadership, marketing, etc. As you achieve your dreams, industry associations will then afford you the opportunity to assist the next generation of dreamers who follow behind you.

Once you reach your new level—once you're living in freedom—as God's servant, you must expand your associations to others who need your help. Jesus tells us, "You are the light of the world. A city that is set on a hill cannot be hidden."[2] When you're pregnant in your faith and in your dream, you climb that hill, but after you arrive, you need to shine your light. "Let your light so shine before men, that they may see your good works and glorify your Father in heaven."[3]

God must get the glory for the works He does through us, and for Him to get the glory, we need to tell our story. We shouldn't be the spotlight, we should simply be the light. Once we see our vision come true, we must testify to the world of His amazing wonders. God gets all the glory.

Go and Live!

The associations we make, the ownership we take, the passion we pursue, the purpose we fulfill, the vision we see, the faith we follow—these will give us the life we want. These will move us to living in freedom everyday.

Our destiny is to "have life" and "have it more abundantly." Jesus lived, died, and rose, so we could break off the shackles that bind us in slavery. The job, the money, the lifestyle that hold us in bondage—they are imposters, keeping us in the stuck position only because we don't know how to move forward.

But if we haven't known how to move forward before, now we do. The keys are in this book, and now it's your time.

It *is* your time.

It is your time to look inside yourself. It is your time to become the masterpiece God created. It is your time to experience, not mere happiness, but everlasting joy.

It is your time to pursue success. The fact that you've acquired this book and read it tells you that you're ready. It tells you that you've taken the first step along the journey of success. You've started. There's no looking back now. There's no need to hesitate.

The Lord has put you on this earth as part of a mighty orchestra. You have a part to play. The music you play will be glorious. And it will ignite the heavens with rejoicing and celebration.

Go out and play the part you were born to play. Go out and live your making.

Go out and live in freedom every day.

(Footnotes)
[1] Matthew 5:14
[2] Matthew 5:16

If you need further assistance,
feel free to contact me at:
livinginfreedomeveryday.com

– ABOUT THE AUTHOR –
Kenneth Brown

Kenneth Brown is the owner and operator of a successful McDonald's restaurant in the Metro-Detroit area.

Ken began his career with ARA Services — a food management company. During his tenure as assistant director of Food Service, Ken developed a passion for leadership and excellence. Ken spent the next 12 years working in many facets of the food service industry. He has held many positions including general manager for Wendy's, sales manager for Kraft Foods and sales consultant for The Assmussen Waxler Group and McDonald's Corporation.

Ken is a native of Chicago, Illinois and is a graduate of Southern Illinois University.

Ken Brown's life story is included in "Keeping the Faith - Stories of Courage, Healing and Hope for Black America," a collection of inspirational biographies compiled by journalist and talk show host Tavis Smiley.

To contact Kenneth Brown for booksignings, speaking engagements or to order more copies of this book — call **248.669.6614**, send an E-mail to **Ken@kenbrowninternational.com** or visit his website at *www.kenbrowninternational.com*